LITERATURE MADE EASY

EMILY BRONTË'S

WUTHERING HEIGHTS

Written by JANE EASTON
WITH TONY BUZAN

BARRON'S

First edition for the United States and Canada published by Barron's
Educational Series, Inc., 1999

First published in the United Kingdom by Hodder & Stoughton Ltd.
under the title: *Teach Yourself Literature Guides: A Guide to
Wuthering Heights*

Cover photograph © The Ronald Grant Archive
Mind Maps: Anne Jones
Illustrations: Karen Donnelly

Jane Easton asserts the moral right to be identified as the
author of this work.

American text edited by Elizabeth Schmid

All inquiries should be addressed to:
Barron's Educational Series, Inc.
250 Wireless Boulevard
Hauppauge, New York 11788
http://www.barronseduc.com

International Standard Book No. 0-7641-0829-8

Library of Congress Catalog Card No. 98-74654

Printed in the United States of America
9 8 7 6 5 4 3 2 1

CONTENTS

How to study   v

How to use this guide   ix

Key to icons   xi

Background   1
- Family background   1
- Historical background   2
- Literary background   3

The story of *Wuthering Heights*   4

Who's who?   9
- Mr. Earnshaw   10
- Joseph   10
- Heathcliff   10
- Catherine Earnshaw   10
- Hindley Earnshaw   12
- Edgar Linton   12
- Isabella Linton   12
- Nelly Dean   14
- Cathy Linton   14
- Hareton Earnshaw   16
- Linton Heathcliff   16
- Lockwood   16

Themes and Imagery   17
- Love   17
- Imprisonment and freedom   18
- Nature   18
- Outsiders   19
- Childhood   19
- Death and sleep   19

- Social class   20
- Books   21
- Religion   21
- The supernatural   21

Commentary   **25**

- Chapters 1–3   26
- Chapters 4–7   30
- Chapters 8–12   35
- Chapters 13–17   44
- Chapters 18–20   52
- Chapters 21–28   55
- Chapters 29–34   64

Topics for discussion and brainstorming   **72**

How to get an "A" in English Literature   **74**

The exam essay   **76**

Model answer and essay plan   **77**

Glossary of literary terms   **81**

Index   **83**

There are five important things you must know about your brain and memory to revolutionize
the way you study:

◆ how your memory
  ("recall") works *while* you are learning
◆ how your memory works *after* you have finished learning
◆ how to use Mind Maps – a special technique for helping you
  with all aspects of your studies
◆ how to prepare for tests and exams.

Recall during learning
– THE NEED FOR BREAKS

When you are studying, your memory
can concentrate, understand, and
remember well for between 20 and 45
minutes at a time, then it needs a break.
If you continue for longer than this
without a break, your memory starts to
break down. If you study for hours nonstop, you will remember
only a small fraction of what you have been trying to learn, and
you will have wasted hours of valuable time.

So, ideally, *study for less than an hour*, then take a five- to ten-
minute break. During the break listen to music, go for a walk, do
some exercise, or just daydream. (Daydreaming is a necessary
brain-power booster – geniuses do it regularly.) During the break
your brain will be sorting out what it has been learning, and you
will go back to your books with the new information safely
stored and organized in your memory. We recommend breaks
at regular intervals as you work through the Literature Guides.
Make sure you take them!

Recall after learning
– THE WAVES OF YOUR MEMORY

What do you think begins to happen to your memory right after you have finished learning something? Does it immediately start forgetting? No! Your brain actually *increases* its power and continues remembering. For a short time after your study session, your brain integrates the information, making a more complete picture of everything it has just learned. Only then does the rapid decline in memory begin, and as much as 80 percent of what you have learned can be forgotten in a day.

However, if you catch the top of the wave of your memory, and briefly review (look back over) what you have been studying at the right time, the memory is imprinted far more strongly, and stays at the crest of the wave for a much longer time. To maximize your brain's power to remember, take a few minutes at the end of a day and use a Mind Map to review what you have learned. Then review it at the end of a week, again at the end of a month, and finally a week before your test or exam. That way you'll ride your memory wave all the way there – and beyond!

The Mind Map ®
– A PICTURE OF THE WAY YOU THINK

Do you like taking notes? More important, do you like having to go back over and learn them before tests or exams? Most students I know certainly do not! And how do you take your notes? Most people take notes on lined paper, using blue or black ink. The result, visually, is boring. And what does *your* brain do when it is bored? It turns off, tunes out, and goes to sleep! Add a dash of color, rhythm, imagination, and the whole note-taking process becomes much more fun, uses more of your brain's abilities, and improves your recall and understanding.

Generally, your Mind Map is highly personal and need not be understandable to any other person. It mirrors *your* brain. Its purpose is to build up your "memory muscle" by creating images that will help you recall instantly the most important points about the characters and plot sequences in a work of fiction you are studying.

You will find Mind Maps throughout this book. Study them, add some color, personalize them, and then try drawing your own – you'll remember them far better. Stick them in your files and on your walls for a quick-and-easy review of the topic.

HOW TO DRAW A MIND MAP

1 First of all, briefly examine the Mind Maps and Mini Mind Maps used in this book. What are the common characteristics? All of them use small pictures or symbols, with words branching out from the illustration.

2 Decide which idea or character in the book you want to illustrate and draw a picture, starting in the middle of the page so that you have plenty of room to branch out. Remember that no one expects a young Rembrandt or Picasso here; artistic ability is not as important as creating an image you (and you alone) will remember. A round smiling (or sad) face might work as well in your memory as a finished portrait. Use marking pens of different colors to make your Mind Map as vivid and memorable as possible.

3 As your thoughts flow freely, add descriptive words and other ideas on the colored branching lines that connect to the central image. Print clearly, using one word per line if possible.

4 Further refine your thinking by adding smaller branching lines, containing less important facts and ideas, to the main points.

5 Presto! You have a personal outline of your thoughts about the character and plot. It's not a stiff formal outline, but a colorful image that will stick in your mind, it is hoped, throughout classroom discussions and final exams.

HOW TO READ A MIND MAP

1 Begin in the center, the focus of your topic.
2 The words/images attached to the center are like chapter headings; read them next.
3 Always read from the center, in every direction (even on the left-hand side, where you will have to read from right to left, instead of the usual left to right).

USING MIND MAPS

Mind Maps are a versatile tool – use them for taking notes in class or from books, for solving problems, for brainstorming with friends, and for reviewing and working for tests or exams – their uses are endless! You will find them invaluable for planning essays for coursework and exams. Number your main branches in the order in which you want to use them and off you go – the main headings for your essay are done and all your ideas are logically organized!

Preparing for tests and exams

◆ Review your work systematically. Study hard at the start of your course, not the end, and avoid "exam panic."
◆ Use Mind Maps throughout your course, and build a Master Mind Map for each subject – a giant Mind Map that summarizes everything you know about the subject.
◆ Use memory techniques such as mnemonics (verses or systems for remembering things like dates and events).
◆ Get together with one or two friends to study, compare Mind Maps, and discuss topics.

AND FINALLY...

Have *fun* while you learn – it has been shown that students who make their studies enjoyable understand and remember everything better and get the highest grades. I wish you and your brain every success!

(Tony Buzan)

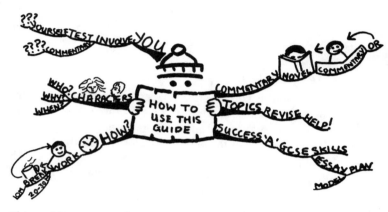

This guide assumes that you have already read *Wuthering Heights*, although you could read Background and The Story of *Wuthering Heights* before that. It is best to use the guide alongside the novel. You could read the Who's Who? and Themes sections without referring to the novel, but you will get more out of these sections if you do refer to it to check the points made in these sections, and especially when thinking about the questions designed to test your recall and help you think about the novel.

The Commentary section can be used in a number of ways. One way is to read a chapter or part of a chapter in the novel, and then read the Commentary for that section. Continue until you come to a test section, test yourself – then take a break. Or, read the Commentary for a chapter, then read that section in the novel, then go back to the Commentary. Find out what works best for you.

Topics for Discussion and Brainstorming gives topics that could well appear on exams or provide the basis for coursework. It would be particularly useful for you to discuss them with friends, or brainstorm them using Mind Map techniques (see p. vii).

How to get an "A" in English Literature gives valuable advice on what to look for in a text, and what skills you need to develop in order to achieve your personal best.

The Exam Essay is a useful night-before reminder of how to tackle exam questions. The Model Answer and Essay gives an example of an "A"-grade essay and the Mind Map and plan used to write it.

The questions

Whenever you come across a question in the guide with a star ✪ in front of it, think about it for a moment. You could even jot down a few words to focus your mind. There is not usually a "right" answer to these questions; it is important for you to develop your own opinions if you want to get an "A." The Test Yourself sections are designed to take you about 10–20 minutes each, which will be time well spent. Take a short break after each one.

EY TO ICONS

Themes and imagery

A **theme** is an idea explored by an author. **Imagery** refers to the kind of word picture used to make the idea come alive. Particular sorts of images are usually associated with each theme. Whenever a theme is dealt with in the guide, the appropriate icon is used. This means you can find where a theme is just by flicking through the book. Try it now!

Love		Death and sleep	
Imprisonment and freedom		Social class	
Nature		Books	
Outsiders		Religion	
Childhood		The supernatural	

 STYLE AND LANGUAGE

This heading and icon are used in the Commentary wherever there is a special section on the author's choice of words and **imagery**.

BACKGROUND

This chapter is about the historical and social context in which Brontë wrote *Wuthering Heights*. It is important for you to have an understanding of these things, but you must always relate your knowledge of the history to the novel itself.

Family background

Emily Brontë was born in 1818. Her father, Patrick Brontë, became the clergyman at Haworth parsonage in Yorkshire, where Emily lived for most of her life. There were five sisters and one brother. Their mother died when Emily was very small, and two sisters died four years later. The surviving children, Charlotte, Branwell, Emily, and Anne, were brought up by their aunt. They lived a very isolated life as children, and educated themselves by reading widely. The children had vivid imaginations and invented fantasy kingdoms called Angria and Gondal, writing many stories and poems about these places.

Emily spent a short time as a governess and later traveled to Brussels to study languages with her older sister, Charlotte. She returned to Haworth in 1842 and remained there until her death. A collection of her poems was published in 1846, and *Wuthering Heights* was published in 1847. She died of a disease (probably tuberculosis) in 1848, at only 29.

Her brother Branwell was a frustrated painter and writer who turned to alcohol and drugs and eventually died at 31. Anne became well known through her novels *Agnes Grey* and *The Tenant of Wildfell Hall*. Charlotte, the oldest sister, became a successful novelist. *Jane Eyre* and *Villette* are two of her most famous works and these, like Emily's *Wuthering Heights*, are still widely read today.

Historical background

The Brontë children grew up as the Industrial Revolution was changing the face of England, Wales, and Scotland. At the beginning of the nineteenth century, most people still lived and worked in the countryside, but some small towns were growing rapidly. As the century passed, hundreds of thousands of Britons moved to find work in huge, new cities like Birmingham and Manchester. New factories, shipyards, and railroads created enormous wealth for a small group of manufacturers and businesspeople; however, conditions for factory and mine workers were terrible. Even young children worked 12 and 14 hours a day, and families were torn apart by the long hours everyone had to work in order to survive. There was widespread social unrest.

Although the Brontës lived in a quiet country area, they were not far from big, new, industrial towns like Halifax and Bradford. Their everyday lives might not have been touched directly by the Industrial Revolution and social changes in Britain, but they would have known about them from magazines and newspapers.

The characters in *Wuthering Heights* lead lives that have been the same for generations, but there is a hint that things will not stay the same forever. Heathcliff is the intruder, the one who does not fit in, because he is neither a servant, nor a farm worker, nor a rich man's son. We never find out how he made his money during his three-year absence, but it is possible that he was an entrepeneur, a self-made businessman. Later in the novel, he becomes even richer by taking away the inheritances of Hareton and Linton. So, even though he was not originally part of the right social class, he becomes part of it later because of his wealth.

Literary background

The rise of a new middle class meant that many more people could read, and the demand for exciting new forms of writing kept growing. Printing technology made books and magazines much less expensive. Long novels were very popular and were published in three parts like a television serial. Another very popular way to publish novels was in short episodes in magazines. Magazine serials ran much longer, and were something like modern television soap operas, because they tended to end on a cliffhanger to make readers buy the next edition of the magazine.

There was still great prejudice toward women in nineteenth-century society, and it was unheard of for women to write plays, not to mention more serious works. However, the success of Jane Austen and other female novelists such as Fanny Burney and Maria Edgeworth made serious writing more "respectable." It meant that the Brontë sisters had a chance of having their novels published, although they took the precaution of writing under male pen names at first. *Wuthering Heights* was published under the name of Ellis Bell, until the real author was discovered to be Emily Brontë. Many critics were shocked that a woman could write about scenes of violence and great emotion, and Emily received some unpleasant criticism (as did the novels of Charlotte and Anne). However, as the century continued, *Wuthering Heights* came to be regarded as an important literary work.

THE STORY OF WUTHERING HEIGHTS

It is 1801. **Lockwood** is the first narrator of the novel. He is a rich young man who has left London to forget a love affair that went wrong. He moves to **Thrushcross Grange** in Yorkshire. Shortly afterward he meets his surly and rather mysterious landlord, **Heathcliff**, who lives at **Wuthering Heights**, an old farmhouse on the moors. Heathcliff lives with a rough-mannered, handsome young man, a grumpy old servant named **Joseph,** and a beautiful but sullen young woman. Lockwood is forced to stay overnight at the Heights and has strange dreams. The last dream is about the ghost of a woman named **Catherine**.

On Lockwood's return to the Grange, the housekeeper, **Nelly Dean**, begins to tell him the story. In 1771 old Mr. **Earnshaw** returns from a business trip to Liverpool with a gypsylike orphan boy named **Heathcliff**. No one knows anything about the child's origins, but Earnshaw's oldest child, **Hindley**, takes an instant dislike to Heathcliff. Earnshaw's daughter, **Catherine**, forms a strong bond with Heathcliff, however, and they roam the **moors** together as children.

When **Earnshaw** dies, **Hindley** treats Heathcliff badly and tries to separate him from **Catherine**. One night, Catherine and Heathcliff wander to **Thrushcross Grange**, where they watch the spoiled **Edgar** and **Isabella Linton** through the window. **Catherine** is rescued from the dogs by the **Lintons** and taken care of, but **Heathcliff** is sent home.

Catherine likes her new life as a young lady, but **Heathcliff's** life is not happy, largely due to Hindley's cruel treatment. Catherine sees more of **Edgar** and is attracted by his good **manners** and wealth. **Catherine** accepts Edgar's proposal of marriage, but also declares her passionate love for **Heathcliff**. Unfortunately, Heathcliff leaves without hearing this, and disappears for **three** years.

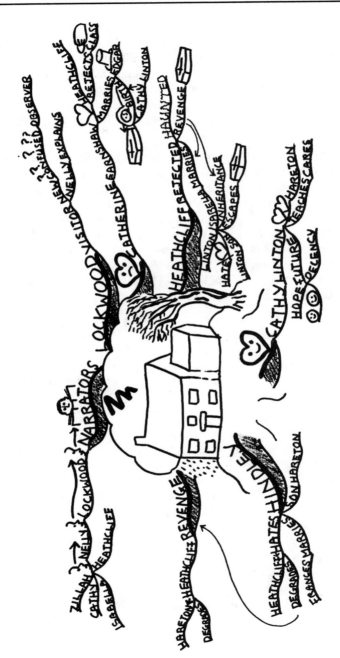

Hindley begins to **drink** after his wife, Frances, **dies**. Only **Nelly** cares for his little son, **Hareton**. Mr. and Mrs. **Linton** die. Edgar and Catherine **marry** and **Nelly** moves to **Thrushcross Grange** to care for the young couple. **Hareton** is now alone with his father, whose drunkenness is worse than ever. **Heathcliff** returns six months after Catherine's marriage and moves into **Wuthering Heights** with **Hindley**, young **Hareton**, and the servant, **Joseph**.

Heathcliff now begins to take revenge on **Hindley**, getting him to **gamble** his money away. He works on degrading **Hareton** by stopping his **education** and ruining his character. **Heathcliff** causes trouble between Edgar and **Catherine**, who becomes very ill after a terrible argument. She **dies** after giving **birth** to her **daughter**, named **Cathy**. In the meantime, **Heathcliff** has eloped with **Isabella** as part of his revenge on the **Linton** family. He treats her with great **cruelty**. After seeing a vicious **fight** between Heathcliff and **Hindley**, she runs away to **London**, where she bears **Linton Heathcliff**, their son.

Heathcliff is beside himself with **grief** after **Catherine's** death, but continues his cruel behavior. He now has **Hindley** and **Hareton** in his power. **Hindley** dies under suspicious circumstances, leaving all his **property** and **land** mortgaged to Heathcliff in the form of **gambling** debts. Heathcliff now owns **Wuthering Heights**.

After **Isabella's** death, her son, **Linton**, is returned to **Heathcliff**. Linton is a miserable, **unhealthy** boy and Heathcliff **mistreats** him. Young **Cathy**, now 16, forms a relationship with **Linton**, but Heathcliff catches her and forces the young couple into **marriage** so he can **inherit** Isabella's property. **Edgar Linton** dies and **Cathy** is left penniless. **Linton** dies soon afterward. Heathcliff now owns all the property and lands of the **Linton** and **Earnshaw** families. He also **controls** the lives of **Hareton** and Cathy, but his **bitterness** begins to fade and he grows **obsessed** with the idea of being united with his **Catherine** once more. He **dies**, leaving Hareton and young Cathy to find **happiness** and the chance of a new **beginning** for themselves and their **descendants**.

HOW MUCH CAN YOU REMEMBER?

Try to fill in the missing words from this summary without looking back at the original. Feel free to use your own words if they have the same meaning.

It is 1801. _____ is the first narrator of the novel. He is a rich young man who has left London to try to forget a love affair that went wrong. He moves to _____ in Yorkshire. Shortly afterward, he meets his surly and rather mysterious landlord, _____ who lives at _____ , an old farmhouse on the moors. Heathcliff lives with a rough-mannered, handsome young man, a grumpy old servant named _____ , and a beautiful but sullen young woman. Lockwood is forced to stay overnight at the Heights and has strange dreams. The last dream is about the ghost of a girl named _____ .

On Lockwood's return to the Grange, the housekeeper, _____ , begins to tell him the story. In 1771 old Mr. _____ returns from a business trip in Liverpool with a gypsylike orphan boy named _____ . No one knows anything about the child's origins, but Earnshaw's oldest child, _____ , takes an instant dislike to Heathcliff. Earnshaw's daughter, _____ , forms a strong bond with Heathcliff, however, and they roam the _____ together as children.

When _____ dies, _____ treats Heathcliff badly and tries to separate him from _____ . One night, Catherine and Heathcliff wander to _____ , where they watch the spoiled _____ and _____ through the window. _____ is rescued from the dogs by the _____ and taken care of, but _____ is sent home.

_____ likes her new life as a young lady, but _____'s life is not happy, largely due to Hindley's cruel treatment. Catherine sees more of _____ and is attracted by his good _____ and wealth. _____ accepts Edgar's proposal of marriage, but also declares her passionate love for _____ . Unfortunately, Heathcliff leaves without hearing this, and disappears for _____ years.

_____ begins to _____ after his wife, Frances, _____ . Only _____ cares for his little son,

_____. Mr. and Mrs. _____ die. Edgar and Catherine _____ and _____ move to _____ to care for the young couple. _____ is now alone with his father, whose drunkenness is worse than ever. _____ returns six months after Catherine's marriage and moves into _____ with _____ , young _____, and the servant, _____.

Heathcliff now begins to take revenge on _____ , getting him to _____ his money away. He works on degrading _____ by stopping his _____ and ruining his character. _____ causes trouble between Edgar and _____ , who becomes very ill after a terrible argument. She _____ after giving _____ to her _____ , named _____ . In the meantime, _____ has eloped with _____ as part of his revenge on the _____ family. He treats her with great _____ . After seeing a vicious _____ between Heathcliff and _____ , she runs away to _____ , where she bears _____ , their son.

Heathcliff is beside himself with _____ after _____ death, but continues his cruel behavior. He now has _____ and _____ in his power. _____ dies under suspicious circumstances, leaving all his _____ and _____ mortgaged to Heathcliff in the form of _____ debts. Heathcliff now owns _____ .

After _____ death, her son, _____, is returned to _____ . Linton is a miserable, _____ boy and Heathcliff _____ him. Young _____ , now 16, forms a relationship with _____ , but Heathcliff catches her and forces the young couple into _____ so he can _____ Isabella's property. _____ dies and _____ is left penniless. _____ dies soon afterward. Heathcliff now owns all the property and lands of the _____ and _____ families. He also _____ the lives of _____ and Cathy, but his _____ begins to fade and he grows _____ with the idea of being united with his _____ once more. He _____ , leaving Hareton and young Cathy to find _____ and the chance of a new _____ for themselves and their _____ .

WHO'S WHO?

FAMILY TREE

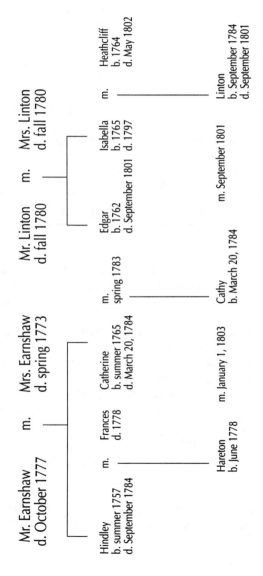

Mr. Earnshaw
d. October 1777

m.

Mrs. Earnshaw
d. spring 1773

Mr. Linton
d. fall 1780

m.

Mrs. Linton
d. fall 1780

Heathcliff
b. 1764
d. May 1802

m.

Hindley
b. summer 1757
d. September 1784

m.

Frances
d. 1778

Catherine
b. summer 1765
d. March 20, 1784

m.
spring 1783

Edgar
b. 1762
d. September 1801

m.

Isabella
b. 1765
d. 1797

Linton
b. September 1784
d. September 1801

Hareton
b. June 1778

m. January 1, 1803

Cathy
b. March 20, 1784

m. September 1801

9

The older generation

MR. EARNSHAW

Earnshaw is Catherine and Hindley's father. Nelly says he has a *kind heart*. He means well by adopting Heathcliff, but does not reassure his own children. He has no patience with Hindley's jealousy and does not understand Catherine's high spirits.

JOSEPH

Joseph is a servant at Wuthering Heights. He thinks of himself as a religious person but is bad tempered and dislikes most people, particularly women. Nelly says he is the *wearisomest, self-righteous pharisee* [religious hypocrite] *that ever ransacked a Bible*. He often stirs up trouble between family members.

The next generation

HEATHCLIFF

Heathcliff is the adopted son of Mr. Earnshaw. He is described as a *cuckoo* because he gradually takes away the inheritances of the Earnshaws and Lintons. Heathcliff is described throughout the novel as *the devil*, and other similar expressions. He is regarded with suspicion by the local people because of his dark, gypsylike appearance. He loves Catherine Earnshaw passionately but Catherine will not marry out of her social class. Heathcliff runs away, returning to take revenge on Hindley and the Lintons. He becomes obsessed with Catherine after her death. (See page 11 for a Mind Map of his character.)

CATHERINE EARNSHAW

Catherine Earnshaw is a powerful character who continues to influence or "haunt" others after her death. As a child, she is mischievous and independent. Nelly describes her as a *wild wick* [lively] *slip ... but she had the bonniest eye and sweetest smile. I believe she meant no harm.* Catherine lives

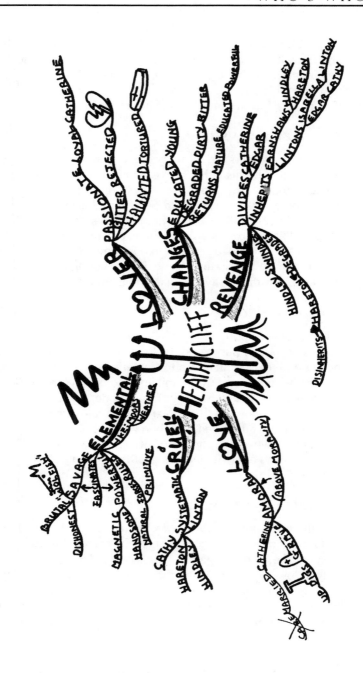

11

by instinct and emotion, not by the usual commonsense rules of life. She is capable of deep love, but can be hurtful to others and finds it difficult to understand people who do not feel as passionately as she. Her decision to marry Edgar places her in an impossible situation, and the strain of it eventually kills her. (See page 13 for a Mind Map of her character.)

HINDLEY EARNSHAW

Hindley is 14 years old at the beginning of Nelly's tale. He feels rejected by his father's love for Heathcliff, especially after being sent away to school. He later stops Heathcliff's education to prevent him from becoming a gentleman and is cruel and neglectful to Catherine. Frances's death tips him into despair. His drunkenness and violence cause Wuthering Heights to have a bad reputation. Hindley ends up penniless and in debt to Heathcliff. His neglect of young Hareton is in strong contrast to the way Edgar brings up Cathy.

EDGAR LINTON

Edgar is first introduced to us by Heathcliff, who describes the boy as weak and pampered. Nelly calls Edgar a *soft thing* because he cannot stand up to Catherine's temper. He does not really understand Catherine and the couple are complete opposites. He tries to live by a moral code, but Catherine and Heathcliff are beyond this. Edgar is a complex character. He can be weak and unkind, as when he rejects his sister, Isabella. However, he shows loyalty and devotion by shaking off depression after Catherine's death and being a good father to young Cathy.

ISABELLA LINTON

Isabella is described as *infantile*. She is no match for Catherine or Heathcliff because she has been so protected from life. Heathcliff uses her to get his hands on the Linton fortune. She falls in love with a romantic dream, not the real Heathcliff, although there are hints that she gets a strange enjoyment from his violent ways. However, she shows some spirit when she runs away to find a new life.

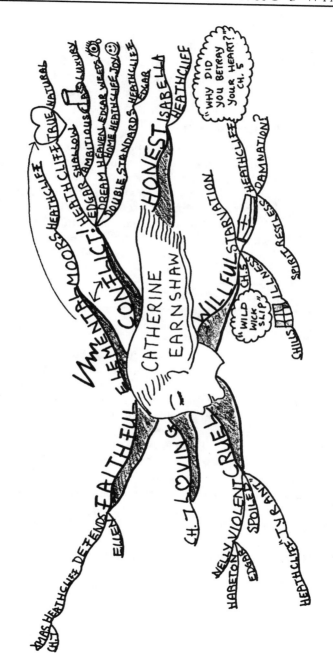

13

NELLY DEAN

Nelly Dean (Ellen) is the main narrator of the novel, and it is through her that we see most of the action. She is a hard-working, honest, and loyal woman who is not afraid to give her opinion. She shows great common sense, but even she sometimes misjudges situations, as when she ignores Catherine's illness in Chapter 11.

Nelly is well educated for her time, but has wisdom and common sense, not just book learning. Many characters confide in her, showing that she is regarded as trustworthy. She is brave, but sometimes it seems as if she is too used to violence, because she often describes terrible scenes in a very matter-of-fact way. We see her contentment at the end of the novel, as the marriage of her two beloved *nurslings* grows nearer, and happiness returns to Wuthering Heights.

The new generation

CATHY LINTON

Cathy is the daughter of Catherine and Edgar. When Lockwood first meets her, she seems to resemble the worst side of her mother. *She flung the tea back ... and resumed her chair in a pet ... her red underlip pushed out, like a child's, ready to cry.* This description shows Heathcliff's power to change even the most loving nature. Later, Nelly shows us the real Cathy, whose heart is sensitive and lively and whose love is never fierce but deep and tender. Cathy can be cruel and thoughtless, as when she mocks Hareton's efforts to read, yet she is truly shocked by hearing about Heathcliff's evil deeds. She is very loyal to Linton, despite his ungrateful behavior, and her loving nature helps to mend the quarrel between herself and Hareton. This is the beginning of hope for the new generation. (See page 15 for a Mind Map of her character.)

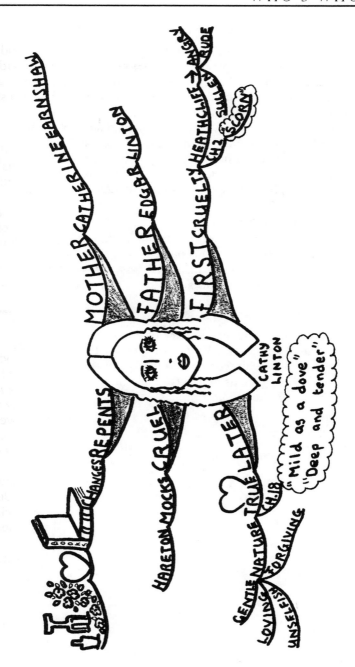

HARETON EARNSHAW

Hareton is Hindley's son and is hated by Heathcliff for this reason. Hareton becomes a terrible echo of Heathcliff's own degradation by Hindley. Like Heathcliff, he is handsome and intelligent, but is made to seem like little more than an animal. He is illiterate and foul-mouthed, and is encouraged to think of anything fine as worthless and *soft*. Hareton's instinctive love of beauty makes him change. Books are a way to improve his life and bring him closer to Cathy. He even shows love and forgiveness toward Heathcliff, and it is these qualities that help to bring about the new beginning at Wuthering Heights.

LINTON HEATHCLIFF

The son of Isabella and Heathcliff, Linton is a weak, sickly boy with a vicious side to his nature. Only Cathy loves and cares for him. Nelly dislikes his selfishness. He is despised by his father, who uses him to get at Cathy's inheritance.

LOCKWOOD

Lockwood is the first narrator of the novel. He is not a good judge of character and finds making relationships difficult, particularly with women. He is a rather snobbish, lonely man who always seems to be watching the lives of others, never being a part of things.

THEMES AND IMAGERY

Themes

A theme is an idea developed or explored throughout a work (as in a play, book, or poem). The main themes of *Wuthering Heights* are shown on the Mini Mind Map above, and can be identified as follows:

- love
- imprisonment and freedom
- nature
- outsiders
- childhood
- death and sleep
- social class
- books
- religion
- the supernatural

Love

Romantic love is difficult for every character in the novel, even though *Wuthering Heights* is often thought of as a love story. Every relationship but one is ruined by death or separation. Only Cathy and Hareton are given the chance for a happy, fruitful marriage.

Family love is also shown in a variety of ways. Relationships between family members are often marked by jealousy, cruelty, or neglect. Even in supposedly happy families like the Lintons, the children seem spoiled and overprotected. Yet there are times when the family provides affection and love, as in the relationship between Edgar Linton and his daughter, Cathy. Nelly is also an important provider of family love, even though she is not related by blood to any of the characters.

Imprisonment and freedom

Throughout the novel, characters are often "locked up," either physically or emotionally. This imprisonment might be caused by another person, such as when Heathcliff imprisons Isabella and Nelly, or it might be caused by the harsh weather, as when Lockwood cannot leave because of the snow. Edgar wants to protect Cathy, so he stops her from going off the grounds of Thrushcross Grange, but this is done out of love, not greed or revenge.

Heathcliff and Catherine are free spirits as children. Even beatings cannot keep them imprisoned, and they often run away. Later on, Catherine is often described as sitting beside an open window. This is a sign of her need for freedom from responsibilities, even though she is grown up.

Nature

The changing seasons and weather have a strong effect on characters and events. *Wuthering Heights* was written almost 200 years ago, when there were no cars or televisions and country life was often very lonely. Bad weather could stop all contact with the outside world, and long, dark winters were likely to cause gloom and depression.

Most important, nature is often described in connection with human emotions and activities in the novel, for example, on the night when Heathcliff leaves the Heights. The terrible storm that follows acts as an echo of the strong emotions felt by Catherine and Heathcliff. The freedom-loving young Heathcliff and Catherine are also associated with the descriptions of the untamed moors they roam together.

Outsiders

The country people in the novel are often suspicious and unfriendly toward strangers. Heathcliff is the most important outsider in *Wuthering Heights*, and is treated with prejudice because he is dark-skinned and looks like a gypsy. He is not a natural member of the Earnshaw family but is not a servant either, so people do not know how to place him.

Lockwood does not fit in because he is a rich southerner and a stranger to the area. Heathcliff treats his own son, Linton, as if he were an outsider.

Childhood

The world of childhood is important to the novel. Children were treated more rigidly than is usual today. Although poor children would have been working from an early age, rich children like Catherine and the Lintons were usually overprotected. However, many of the children in *Wuthering Heights* experience unusual levels of cruelty and neglect.

We meet almost all the major characters as children and follow them into adulthood. Emily Brontë has a great understanding about the way children think and behave. She writes about Hindley's treatment of the young Heathcliff and Catherine with sympathy. She is not sentimental about children, however, and understands that they can be cruel and jealous as well as funny and kind. For example, the description of young Hareton hanging puppies is shocking but believable, while Catherine dancing outside the door of the Heights creates an amusing picture of a lively, energetic girl.

Death and sleep

Early death was much more common in the nineteenth century than today. Women were more likely to die in childbirth, and many diseases that are curable today were killers then. Emily Brontë knew this from personal experience after the deaths of her mother, two sisters, and a brother.

There are many deaths in the novel. What is especially important is the way in which the dead have such a powerful effect on the living; for example, Catherine's influence after death continues to affect others, especially Heathcliff. Even Lockwood, who knows nothing about her, is "haunted" by her in a dream. When Mr. Earnshaw dies, Heathcliff is no longer protected from Hindley's hatred, and Hindley destroys Heathcliff's life after Hindley loses his wife.

Sleep and death are often described in a very similar way; for instance, Lockwood gets into the coffinlike closet bed and dreams about Catherine, a dead woman. Another example is Linton, who would rather stay in bed than go outside. This is a hint that he already believes himself to be close to the coffin and death.

Social class

At the beginning of the nineteenth century, it was difficult to move out of the class into which one was born. Nelly is unusual because she is well educated for a servant. Although servants were sometimes treated almost as family members, as Nelly and Joseph were, they were expected to know their place.

The way characters speak (**accent** and **dialect**) is used to show the difference in social class. Cathy cannot believe that Hareton is a relative of hers because he speaks like a farm worker. Level of education is also an important difference between the classes. Many of the poorer people would have been virtually illiterate (unable to read or write). Hindley stops Heathcliff's education in order to prevent him from improving his chances in life.

Heathcliff is unusual because he is not a servant nor has he inherited money like the Earnshaws and Lintons. He returns wealthy after a three-year absence, but no one knows how he has earned his money. He despises the pampered Lintons, who do not work for a living but, ironically, he becomes a rich landowner himself after inheriting the Linton and Earnshaw properties.

Books

Books are mentioned frequently throughout the novel. People like Lockwood, the Lintons, and Earnshaws would have had a lot of spare time, so reading was an important leisure activity.

Books are used in different ways: Lockwood uses them to escape reality and to relieve boredom, Joseph uses religious books to control the children, and books unite Hareton and Cathy.

One of the most important differences between Catherine and Edgar is described in terms of books. Catherine and Heathcliff represent strong emotion, whereas Edgar is part of the world of reason and controlled feelings. After a terrible argument involving Catherine, Edgar, and Heathcliff, Edgar goes to his library. Catherine cannot believe this: *What in the name of all that feels, has he to do with books when I am dying?*

Religion

Nearly everyone in the Brontës' time would have been a Christian, and most people went to church or chapel. The author herself was a parson's daughter, yet there seems to be a criticism of religion in the novel. Most of this comes through Joseph, who is portrayed as a spiteful hypocrite. He uses Christianity to tell people that they are sinners going to hell, instead of concentrating on love and peace.

Wuthering Heights does not say much about God, which is unusual for a nineteenth-century novel. Heathcliff and Catherine seem to worship nature more than God, which would have been shocking to many readers at that time.

The supernatural

Wuthering Heights contains a strong supernatural element. Catherine's ghost is described many times, and Heathcliff is believed to haunt the moors after his death. Local fairy tales and superstitions are also featured, as Joseph frequently refers to Catherine and Cathy as *witches* who put spells on men. Nelly herself mentions local songs and stories about fairies.

21

Imagery

Imagery is language used to compare something and make us see it more vividly; for example, Catherine describes her love for Edgar Linton as *foliage in the woods* because it will eventually fade and die, like leaves on trees. She describes her love for Heathcliff as *the eternal rocks beneath*, because she believes her love for him is as necessary and everlasting as the ground we walk on.

Symbolism

Symbolism is the use of an object to represent something else; for example, a dove can mean peace, a rose may mean love. In *Wuthering Heights*, windows and doors are described as real objects, of course, but they are mentioned so many times that they stand for more than just parts of a house. Characters sometimes smash down doors as a way of getting at someone, or to escape from someone. Sometimes, open windows symbolize a character's need for freedom.

Style

Style is the way an author writes, his or her individual "signature"; for example, Emily Brontë uses many narrators, as well as moving the story backward and forward in time with the use of flashback. She uses imagery connected to nature, as mentioned earlier.

Another important feature of Brontë's style is her use of repetition. We often get confused about the characters because their names are identical or similar. Brontë does this to show how each generation is strongly influenced by the actions of the generation before them. Will they make the same mistakes? Will they be able to change the course of events or not?

Heathcliff and Catherine's relationship comes to nothing. Hareton and Cathy have similar names, but they succeed. The first generation does not make the right choices, whereas Cathy overcomes her false pride and Hareton improves himself. And Linton and Cathy's relationship is doomed, not just because Linton is so ill, but because he represents the

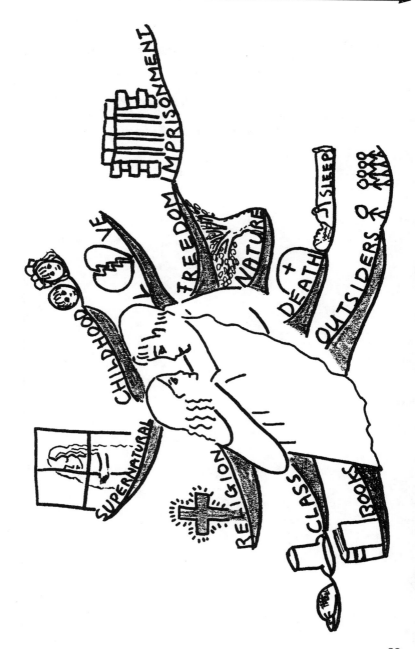

worst combination of the Linton family and Heathcliff. This is emphasized by the two parts of his name: Linton, for the weak, spoiled aspects of that family, and Heathcliff for the vicious and manipulative side. Cathy, on the other hand, inherits all the best qualities of her mother and father, and has a loving and supportive upbringing. Hareton has a similar upbringing to Heathcliff, but instead of being dragged down by bitterness and revenge, he makes a fresh start.

COMMENTARY

To make review easier, the Commentary divides the novel into sections beginning with a brief preview that will prepare you for the section and help with last-minute review. The Commentary discusses whatever is important in the section, focusing on the areas shown in the Mini Mind Map above.

ICONS

Wherever there is a focus on a particular theme, the icon for that theme appears in the margin (see p. xi for key). Look out, too, for the Style and Language sections. Being able to comment on style and language will help you to get an "A" on your exam.

You will learn more from the Commentary if you use it alongside the novel itself. Read a section from the novel, then the corresponding Commentary section – or the other way around.

STARRED QUESTIONS

Remember that whenever a question appears in the Commentary with a star ✪ in front of it, you should stop and think about it for a moment. And **do remember to take a break** after completing each exercise.

Section 1 Chapters 1–3

CHAPTER *1*

◆ November 1801: Lockwood moves to Thrushcross Grange
◆ He meets Heathcliff, his landlord
◆ Lockwood is unwelcome at Wuthering Heights

Lockwood is a rich young gentleman from the south of England who has moved to Thrushcross Grange, a mansion on the Yorkshire Moors. He describes the first meeting with his landlord, Heathcliff, at Wuthering Heights, Heathcliff's farmhouse. Although Heathcliff is rude and unwelcoming, Lockwood enters the farm. His thoughts take him back to the broken love affair that caused him to move to Yorkshire. ❂Why do you think he behaves like this toward the young woman whom he met on vacation? He then returns to the main story, at which point he is attacked by the dogs in the kitchen. Neither Heathcliff nor Joseph seems to care. Despite their treatment of him, Lockwood is determined to return the next day. ❂Why does he want to visit such unfriendly people again?

✒ STYLE AND LANGUAGE

"Wuthering" is a Yorkshire expression for stormy, rather like the strong emotions of the people who live there. Brontë also describes *stunted firs* and *gaunt thorns* near the farmhouse, which seem similar to the emotional state of the characters living there. Their lives are so bitter and unhappy they are unable to "grow." The house itself is described as a fortress with its narrow windows and corners *defended* with large jutting stones. This suggests the suspicion of strangers that is shown to Lockwood.

 Lockwood is an outsider because he is a southerner and a visitor. He is frightened of romantic relationships and so stays away from them. Heathcliff is also an outsider, but for different reasons. Brontë immediately introduces the contradictory side to Heathcliff's character by describing him as both a *gentleman* and a *gypsy*.

CHAPTER 2

- November 1801, the following day: Lockwood visits the Heights again
- He meets Hareton and Cathy
- He is trapped by the snow; stays the night

This chapter sets the scene for the tangle of relationships that is such a strong feature of the novel. Lockwood is confused by Heathcliff, Hareton, and Cathy, and so is the reader. In addition, Lockwood's experiences in the area are unfriendly. He is not made welcome by the servants at Thrushcross Grange, so he walks to Wuthering Heights in the freezing cold. Even the weather is hostile, and Joseph is unwilling to let him in. He gets his first glimpse of how brutal life is at the Heights in the way that Heathcliff responds to Cathy.

No one will help him to get home safely, and even worse, when he takes a lantern to guide himself, Joseph sets the dogs on him. Lockwood is shocked and hurt, so Heathcliff grudgingly allows him to stay the night.

Despite the strange behavior of the people there, the kitchen is warm and cozy. Brontë often describes very ordinary, pleasant domestic surroundings, even though the characters may be in an emotional upheaval. This helps to make the novel more down to earth and believable.

Lockwood wants to escape the unpleasant atmosphere at the Heights, but the weather keeps him a prisoner.

Lockwood is puzzled by Hareton, who has rough manners and a workman's hands, yet does not act like a servant. He cannot place him socially and manages to irritate the young man. ◐Why does Lockwood need to find out Hareton's identity and social class?

CHAPTER 3

- Lockwood sleeps in a closet bed
- He finds Catherine's diary

- He dreams about a sermon, then about Catherine
- He wakes Heathcliff
- He walks back to the Grange in the snow

This is a very important chapter in the novel. Lockwood learns some facts about the family from Catherine's diary, which is another form of narrator.

Lockwood is hidden in the closet bed, and reads the diary, which is written in a religious book. He has two vivid dreams. The first is about a long sermon in a church; the second is a nightmare that Catherine's ghost is crying to be let in from the cold. He is so frightened in this dream that he tries to cut her wrist on the broken glass to stop her from coming through the window. His shouting wakes Heathcliff, who is first of all angry to find him there and then shocked to hear him mention Catherine. Lockwood and the reader get a glimpse of the strong emotions that rule Heathcliff, as he breaks down and begs the dead Catherine to return. The use of dreams and ghosts gives a sense of the overpowering, uncontrollable relationship once shared by the lovers.

There is further confusion when Lockwood gets lost in the snow on his way back home the following day.

The weather is harsh and changeable, rather like the emotions in this chapter. Lockwood is confused and frightened by his experiences at the Heights, just as he gets lost in the snow later. It is as if he cannot be sure of anything in this strange place.

Both Catherine's diary and Lockwood's dream about Jabes Branderham describe religion as something used as a punishment. In addition, Catherine's diary is written in a religious book, which shows her lack of respect for conventional religion.

The closet bed is like a coffin, and the idea of death is emphasized by Lockwood dreaming of the dead Catherine.

Questions to ask yourself

? Why does Lockwood try to push Catherine away by hurting her in the dream?

? Does this remind you of his actions at another time? Look back to Chapter 1 and compare the two events. What do they tell us about his relationships with women?

now take a break before reading about family jealousy, a religious bigot – and death

November 1801, Lockwood arrives at Thrushcross Grange, unwelcomed and confused by Heathcliff and the strange household at Wuthering Heights. He dreams about a dead girl whom he has never met.

Section 2 Chapters 4–7

CHAPTER 4

◆ Nelly begins her narration; we go back in time to about 1771
◆ Mr. Earnshaw takes a trip to Liverpool; he returns with Heathcliff
◆ Anger and jealousy among the children

The return of Mr. Earnshaw from Liverpool with an orphan boy causes trouble in the family. Catherine and Hindley are upset because their father seems to have forgotten or broken their presents for the sake of the strange child. Heathcliff looks like a gypsy, does not speak English, and is described right from the start as an "intruder." He also seems *hardened* and *insensible* to kindness or cruelty, which introduces the reader to the bad side of his character. Nelly also dislikes him, although Catherine soon makes friends with the new boy. Hindley hates him, however. ✪What is Hindley so afraid of? What does he mean when he calls Heathliff a *beggarly interloper?*

We see the calculating side of Heathcliff when he blackmails Hindley by threatening to tell Mr. Earnshaw about his beatings. Hindley does exchange his horse as Heathcliff orders, but still attacks Heathcliff. Nelly says that, although she did not believe Heathcliff was vindictive, she later realized that she was completely wrong. This suggests that Heathcliff will eventually get his revenge. Brontë is setting the scene for what Heathcliff does later in the novel.

We are not given a picture of childhood happiness here. Instead, the children are violent and jealous, yet Heathcliff is cool and strangely without emotion for such a young boy.

Heathcliff is very much the outsider, sometimes described as *it* instead of "he" and as an *interloper*. His inability to speak English and his dark coloring also make the household prejudiced and suspicious of him. ✪Why does Nelly say that the history of his life is a *cuckoo's?*

CHAPTER 5

- ◆ 1771–77: Mr. Earnshaw becomes ill
- ◆ Hindley behaves badly; he and his father clash
- ◆ Hindley is sent away to school
- ◆ Earnshaw dies, October 1777

Mr. Earnshaw's health begins to fail. This is one of the many examples of illness and decay and death that are repeated throughout the novel. He and Hindley clash, not helped by Joseph's interfering ways. Catherine is misunderstood by her father also, which makes her behave badly. She is, however, extremely upset when Earnshaw dies in front of the fire one stormy October evening. Nelly later sees the two children comforting each other and wishes they could all be safe in heaven. ❶Why does Brontë describe a storm at the time of Earnshaw's death? What is this literary device called?

Mr. Earnshaw's death makes Catherine and Hindley orphans. It also represents the end of Heathcliff's protection and security, although we do not know this yet.

Joseph uses his knowledge to influence Mr. Earnshaw and turn him against the children. Once again, religion is used to punish, instead of to help.

Understanding Catherine

? Remind yourself of the description of Catherine. (*Certainly, she had ways with her ... beg to be forgiven*). Make a Mini Mind Map, using key words that describe her character. What do you think of her?

? Add to the Mind Map after you have read Chapter 8 and see if your opinion has changed.

next, family violence and an adventure at Thrushcross Grange—but take a break first

CHAPTER 6

- ◆ 1797: Hindley, now the master of the house, returns home with a wife, Frances
- ◆ Hindley begins Heathcliff's "degradation"
- ◆ Heathcliff takes on the role of narrator to Nelly, describing his and Catherine's adventures at Thrushcross Grange
- ◆ Hindley orders Heathcliff to stay away from Catherine

This is another key chapter in the novel, as it sows the seeds for the divisions that grow between Catherine and Heathcliff. It also shows the beginning of Heathcliff's degradation by Hindley.

Nonetheless, Hindley's cruelty brings Catherine and Heathcliff closer together at first. He stops Heathcliff's education and makes him work as a farm laborer. Heathcliff and Catherine frequently run off to escape Joseph and Hindley, and Nelly describes the children as *unfriended creatures.*

One Sunday evening, the children are caught peering through the windows into Thrushcross Grange, home of the Linton family. They are so unwanted by their own family that they are amazed to see the beautiful, luxurious surroundings. But the spoiled young Edgar and Isabella are bad-tempered in spite of being so well cared for, and are quarreling over a dog. Heathcliff despises the brother and sister right from the beginning, which prepares us for his behavior later in the novel.

Heathcliff returns to tell the Earnshaws that Catherine is safe at the Grange. The following day, Mr. Linton visits the Heights and lectures Hindley about the lack of guidance he is giving Catherine. Hindley warns Heathcliff to keep away from her.

Nelly does not realize it, but Frances has a serious illness that will eventually kill her. Brontë emphasizes the frequency of death by describing a dying woman at a funeral.

Hindley stops Heathcliff's education because he is deliberately trying to make sure that Heathcliff never becomes a "gentleman." Heathcliff also has to work outside like a farmhand, something that middle-class and upper-class people did not do.

The incident at the Grange further emphasizes the class differences between Catherine and Heathcliff. Catherine is allowed to stay there and is treated like a princess. Heathcliff tells Nelly that Catherine *is a young lady and they made a distinction between her treatment and mine.* In fact, the Lintons assume that Heathcliff is a thief because of his dark coloring.

Over to you

? Remind yourself of the descriptions of Edgar and Isabella in this chapter. Make a Mind Map, comparing them with Catherine.

? Make a list of the reasons why Heathcliff is so scornful of the young Lintons.

now take a break. Then find out if the unkempt Heathcliff has a chance with the new, elegant Catherine

CHAPTER 7

◆ Christmas 1777: Catherine returns to Wuthering Heights as a young lady
◆ Heathcliff is more neglected and dirty
◆ Heathcliff attacks Edgar; he swears revenge on Hindley
◆ Nelly's narration stops temporarily and she and Lockwood chat

Catherine returns. Not only is she beautifully dressed, but she behaves in a much calmer and more polite way. ✪Why does Heathcliff behave so awkwardly toward her now?

The contrast between Heathcliff and her is painful. Hindley enjoys humiliating the boy. He treats him like one of the servants.

Despite this, Nelly encourages Heathcliff to clean himself up and he promises to be good. He is jealous of Edgar Linton's blond good looks and the wealth he will inherit, as he thinks these things will make Catherine prefer Edgar. Nelly cheers him up by telling him *a good heart will help you to a bonny face ... you're fit for a prince in disguise.* ✪Is Nelly right? Could Heathcliff have won Catherine's affection by being nicer?

Heathcliff attacks Edgar and is beaten and banned from Christmas dinner. ✪Why do you think Catherine is angry at Edgar? Why does she defend Heathcliff?

Although she pretends to be happy, we see the loving side to Catherine when she secretly weeps over Heathcliff's punishment. Nelly and Catherine comfort the beaten boy, who swears revenge on Hindley, despite Nelly's words of warning. Catherine and Heathcliff spend time together, and we get a sense of the strong bond between them.

The narration returns to the present, then Nelly moves the story to the summer of 1778.

Heathcliff is more left out of the family than ever.

Lockwood is a well-educated man, but Nelly Dean is more realistic and has greater common sense than he. She has read widely, but also uses her experience of life to help her to understand people. Books do not always teach wisdom, certainly not in Lockwood's case.

If only ...

? A turning point for Heathcliff comes in this chapter. Where do you think it is?

? Could it have been prevented, or does Heathcliff's character make this bound to happen?

? Write down your opinions in Mind Map form, using quotations from the chapter to prove what you say.

next, Hindley takes to the bottle, while Catherine can't make up her mind. Find out more – after the break

Heathcliff adopted by Mr. Earnshaw. Hatred begins between Heathcliff and Hindley. Growing bond between Catherine and Heathcliff, but Catherine has changed into a lady.

Section 3 Chapters 8–12

CHAPTER 8

- ◆ June 1778: Hareton Earnshaw is born to Hindley and Frances
- ◆ Frances dies soon afterward; Hindley begins to drink and gamble
- ◆ Wuthering Heights loses respectability
- ◆ Catherine is now 15; friendship with Edgar and Heathcliff is difficult
- ◆ Heathcliff's character is worse
- ◆ Edgar experiences Catherine's temper for the first time

Frances dies and Hindley goes downhill fast. Brontë shows here how unstable and unpredictable life is for the characters at Wuthering Heights. We have already met Hareton, an uneducated and surly young man. At this point in the novel we see him as a motherless baby, unwanted by his unhappy and drunken father.

The novel describes scenes of increasing degradation and violence. This family is falling apart. Hindley's treatment of Heathcliff is *enough to make a fiend of a saint*, and indeed, Nelly describes Heathcliff as becoming *diabolical*, or like the devil. No one respectable visits the house anymore, except for Edgar Linton, who is still friendly with Catherine.

Catherine has grown into a beautiful young woman, although she is *haughty and headstrong*. However, Catherine feels confused and full of conflict because Heathcliff and Edgar dislike each other so much. This is the beginning of the great problems in her life. ❍Why does Catherine like each man so much, even though they are complete opposites? Have you ever had problems because of friendships with two very different people?

Brontë shows us how difficult the situation is when Catherine and Heathcliff argue about the "almanack," which is a type of calendar. He has been keeping a record of how much time she spends with Edgar. Catherine is angry and tells him *it's no company at all, when people know nothing and say nothing.* ❍What is she saying about Heathcliff now? Why has he changed so much? When Edgar arrives, Nelly notices a strong difference between the two young men. *The contrast resembled what you see in exchanging a bleak, hilly, coal country for a beautiful fertile valley.*

❍Who is described as the coal country and who is compared to a beautiful valley? What do we learn about Edgar's voice and accent right after this quote? What do you think about the young men now?

Catherine loses her temper after the argument with Heathcliff. She is physically violent. Edgar is shocked by this side of her and tries to leave, but Catherine's tears bring him back. ❍Nelly uses a **simile** to describe Edgar's lack of willpower. Can you find it? Why does she also say Edgar is *doomed*?

At the end of the chapter, Hindley returns home raving drunk, and Nelly takes the bullets out of his gun to protect the household from his rage. This is yet another example of the emotional and physical violence in this chapter. Like death, Nelly describes it in a rather matter-of-fact way, and it is Edgar Linton, not a household member, who seems most shocked by Catherine's behavior. Perhaps Nelly has become hardened because of the constant violence and cruelty at the Heights.

Frances dies, and this affects the entire household, because Hindley is so unhappy that he begins to drink and gamble. Nelly does not spend a lot of time describing the death, which adds to the feeling that it is almost a common event.

The three young people feel love for each other, but none of them seems improved or made happy by it: Heathcliff is sullen and jealous, Catherine is selfish and bad-tempered, and Edgar is weak and under her spell.

Catherine grows up

? Look back at your notes about Catherine from Chapter 5 on. Write a few sentences to explain how she has changed.

a near miss, a mysterious disappearance, and a marriage follow – but for now, take a break

CHAPTER 9

- ◆ 1780: Hareton is rescued from Hindley's violence by Heathcliff
- ◆ Heathcliff longs for Hindley's death
- ◆ Catherine asks Nelly's advice about Edgar's proposal of marriage
- ◆ She compares Heathcliff to Edgar
- ◆ Heathcliff overhears, but misunderstands the conversation; he leaves the Heights

- Catherine has a fever after looking for Heathcliff in a storm
- Mr. and Mrs. Linton die from the fever
- Catherine becomes more moody and bad-tempered
- April 1783: Edgar and Catherine are married; Nelly goes with them to the Grange, leaving young Hareton behind
- Return to Lockwood's narration

This is another key chapter in the novel. It highlights the impossible situation Catherine is in, with regard to Edgar and Heathcliff. It also shows the strength of Heathcliff's feelings toward Hindley. *He expressed ... the intensest anguish at having made himself the instrument of thwarting his own revenge.* ❑What does Brontë mean by this? Why should Heathcliff want Hareton dead?

Catherine seems unsure about her decision to marry Edgar. She does not realize that Heathcliff is listening in the shadows. ❑Why doesn't Nelly warn her?

Catherine describes a dream that she believes means *I've no more business to marry Edgar Linton than I have to be in heaven*, and says that such a marriage would never have crossed her mind if Hindley had not brought Heathcliff so *low*. As she is explaining that it would *degrade* her to marry Heathcliff now, he slips out, believing that she hates him. He misses the rest of her statement, where she declares her feelings for him.❑Why do you think Nelly keeps quiet? Do you agree with what she does?

Catherine will not accept that anything could come between them, even her marriage to Edgar. She says *Nelly, I am Heathcliff.* Nelly does not understand. She tells Catherine that either she does not understand how marriage changes one's life, or that she is a *wicked, unprincipled girl.* ❑Is it possible to break society's rules about love and marriage? Is Catherine selfish or naïve or ... ? What do you think?

The morning after Heathcliff's disappearance, Nelly finds Catherine in the kitchen with the front door and its windows open. ❑Can you explain how this fits in with the windows and doors symbolism in the novel?

We see the effect of the emotional pressure on Catherine, who becomes more irritable and bad-tempered. She marries Edgar three years later and Nelly is forced to go with the young couple to the Grange, leaving little Hareton behind.

Once again, love is not straightforward. Catherine's love for Edgar is shallow, but she is not willing to risk her social position with Heathcliff. She loses her soulmate when he runs away. Catherine takes Nelly's affection for granted and is rude and ungrateful.

The storm is used as a symbol of the emotional tension between Catherine and Heathcliff. The fire is a symbol of the home, and when it is put out by the storm, this suggests that the home is threatened by the violence and quarrels of those who live there.

Torn between two lovers

? Make a chart to show the difference between the descriptions of Heathcliff and Edgar in Chapters 8 and 9.

Some examples have been done for you.

Words used about Edgar	Words used about Heathcliff
foliage in the woods	eternal rocks beneath
moonbeam	lightning

? When you have completed the list:
a) Write a sentence explaining what the words used to describe Edgar make you think about his character. Do the same for Heathcliff.
b) Write your own simile for each man to explain his character, for example, Edgar is like a gentle spring day, Heathcliff is like a blazing summer afternoon.

read on for more scandal. Twisted love and strife – after the break

CHAPTER 10

- ◆ Winter 1801: Lockwood is ill
- ◆ Nelly returns to the story
- ◆ September 1783: Catherine and Edgar are contented, but there are hints of Catherine's despair
- ◆ Heathcliff returns after a three-year absence
- ◆ Catherine's joy, Edgar's jealousy, Nelly's anxiety
- ◆ Isabella falls for Heathcliff; Catherine tries to talk her out of it
- ◆ Hindley's behavior is worse under Heathcliff's influence

Edgar is surprised to see Heathcliff changed into a well-groomed and intelligent-looking man with a dignified manner, instead of the *gypsy, the ploughboy* he remembered, but Nelly thinks she can still see the old wildness in Heathcliff's eyes. Catherine is so excited she does not notice Edgar's jealousy. Heathcliff still harbors violent feelings for Hindley. They act as if Edgar is not there.

Later, Catherine describes how much despair and misery she felt when Heathcliff left; she had even rebelled against God in her anger. ❖Can you see a similarity in the way Catherine speaks about religion in her dream in Chapter 9?

An unexpected twist comes when the 18-year-old Isabella falls in love with Heathcliff. Edgar realizes that although Heathcliff seems changed on the outside, his mind was unchangeable, and unchanged. ❖Remind yourself of the change in Catherine when she returned from the Grange in Chapter 7. Is there a similarity in the way Catherine and Heathcliff have changed?

Catherine warns Isabella about Heathcliff's real nature. ❖What does this tell us about Catherine's love for Heathcliff?

We begin to see that Heathcliff's revenge is taking shape, as Nelly mentions Hindley's increased drinking and gambling.

 **STYLE AND LANGUAGE**

The change that Heathcliff will bring to Edgar and Catherine's marriage is emphasized by the descriptions of him in the shadows. This is a contrast to the fall sunshine described by

Nelly a few sentences before. Heathcliff also looks up at the windows, which reflect the moon but show no light inside. It is as if the house holds no welcome for him; he does not belong there.

Nelly uses a striking image to explain her fears. *I felt that God had forsaken the stray sheep there to its own wicked wanderings, and an evil beast prowled between it and the fold, waiting his time to spring and destroy.* ❍Who is the evil beast; who is the stray sheep?

Despite Heathcliff's transformation into a gentleman, he is still regarded with suspicion. More important, Edgar's worries about Isabella are partly because Heathcliff might be after his family's money. Women had no right to their own money once they were married, so Isabella might be Heathcliff's means of getting at the Linton fortune.

Isabella is young and naïve. Her love is a strong contrast with Catherine and Heathcliff's love.

CHAPTER *11*

- ◆ January 4, 1784: Nelly wants to warn Hindley about Heathcliff
- ◆ Nelly meets young Hareton
- ◆ Heathcliff courts Isabella
- ◆ Catherine and Heathcliff quarrel
- ◆ Edgar steps in; violence between the two men
- ◆ Catherine and Edgar quarrel; she has a breakdown

Nelly visits the Heights, where she meets the foul-mouthed and violent young Hareton. She learns that Heathcliff has stopped the child's education and is encouraging his bad behavior. ❍Why is Heathcliff doing this? Can you explain how this is an example of repetition in the novel?

The discovery of Isabella and Heathcliff kissing provokes a huge fight. Catherine is shocked by Heathcliff's lust for revenge, and is also horrified when he calls her a *tyrant*. It is clear that he is still bitter about her treatment of him when they were younger.

The angry scene involving Heathcliff, Edgar, and Catherine that follows highlights the differences between Edgar's world and the world of Catherine and Heathcliff. Catherine has no illusions about Heathcliff, but is disgusted by Edgar's weakness and emotional coldness. She and Heathcliff take sides, but the conflict triggers Catherine's mental illness. She is unable to cope with the contradictions in her life.

Catherine then has a breakdown, brought about by extreme emotion. Edgar wants her to choose between himself and Heathcliff. Nelly is unsympathetic about her mental state, believing Catherine is just being manipulative.

Catherine throws the door key into the fire because she thinks that Edgar should have the courage to stand up to Heathcliff or else let him go. This is another example of imprisonment.

Edgar is as worried by the idea of Heathcliff inheriting the family fortune as he is by the thought that Isabella might make an unhappy marriage.

Nelly's fears about Hindley's safety at the hands of Heathcliff trigger off some sort of vision. She thinks she sees Hindley as the young boy with whom she used to play.

Spot the difference

? In Chapter 10, Heathcliff describes his hatred of Isabella's eyes. Compare that description with what he says about the vacant blue eyes of the Lintons.

? Now look back at your chart on Heathcliff and Edgar and add details about the difference in their looks.

starvation and family breakdown ... where will it end? But first, take a break

CHAPTER 12

- ◆ Isabella is upset; Edgar escapes in books
- ◆ Catherine starves herself; Nelly does not take her seriously
- ◆ She becomes delirious; Edgar is frightened, then angry with Nelly
- ◆ Catherine rejects Edgar, also Nelly
- ◆ Isabella's dog is hanged by Heathcliff
- ◆ Later, Isabella vanishes; she has eloped with Heathcliff
- ◆ Edgar is finished with his sister

We see how strong the difference between the Lintons and Catherine is in the ways they express their unhappiness. Edgar hides in the library, Isabella is quietly miserable, whereas Catherine becomes ill. ❷What do you think about Nelly's mistrust of Catherine's illness?

Catherine predicts her death. She also says that she is *past wanting* Edgar. This is a sign of how far she is unable to cope with the conflict in her life. Death is a way out of this.

The hanging of Isabella's dog is a symbol of Heathcliff's violent feelings toward her. This incident is especially shocking when we realize that Isabella is going to be married to him. ❷Why does Edgar reject his sister after she elopes with Heathcliff? Do you think he should have done anything else?

Edgar cannot cope with Catherine's extremes of emotion and he retreats to books so he does not have to face up to her anger. For him, his library is an escape from the problems in his relationship. It is another sign of the differences between them.

Catherine's demand for the window to be opened on a winter's day is a sign of how trapped and misunderstood she feels. She also tells stories about the feathers she is tearing from her pillow because they remind her of the birds and moors of her childhood, another example of her need for freedom.

Hindley's behavior goes downhill and he neglects Hareton. Catherine in conflict – Edgar or Heathcliff? Heathcliff leaves. When he returns, Catherine and Edgar are married. Catherine has a breakdown. Isabella elopes. Heathcliff's revenge is beginning to take shape.

Section 4 Chapters 13–17

CHAPTER 13

- Catherine is ill; she is nursed by Edgar
- March 1784: she recovers, but continues to predict her own death; she is pregnant
- Edgar receives an apologetic note from Isabella, but does not reply
- March 13, 1784: Isabella and Heathcliff return to the Heights;
- Nelly receives a letter from Isabella
- Isabella is now the narrator; she describes her terrible life with Heathcliff
- Life at the Heights with Hindley, Heathcliff, Hareton, and Joseph

- Hindley is still having violent urges when he is drunk; he warns Isabella
- Isabella's first night at the Heights; Joseph is unkind and unwelcoming
- Heathcliff's harsh treatment of Isabella; she hates him

Isabella's letter to Nelly gives us another character's viewpoint on how bad life has become at the Heights. Her descriptions of the violence and misery there form a strong contrast with the happy memories Catherine has of her old home. ❂How many examples can you find of the unpleasant conditions and behavior there?

The reader gets an idea of how badly Heathcliff is acting by Isabella's use of **rhetorical questions**. *Is he mad ... is he a devil?* She also asks Nelly *what*, not "who," she has married, which is similar to the way Heathcliff is called *it* earlier in the novel.

Joseph seems to feed on the unhappiness at the house, given his cruel pleasure in Isabella's misery. Despite the difference in accent and social class, he has more control over the household than she does. Heathcliff blames Edgar for Catherine's illness and threatens to take revenge by punishing Isabella.

STYLE AND LANGUAGE

Heathcliff is compared to an animal once more when Isabella says *a tiger or a venomous serpent could not rouse terror in me equal to that which he wakens.*

Another example of style is the state of the house, which is like a reflection of the lives of the people who live there. Heathcliff's bedroom shows signs of violence, with everything torn and broken.

Joseph locks the gate *as if he lived in an ancient castle*, while Hindley warns Isabella to lock her door, to protect herself from his drunken rages. The inhabitants are also imprisoned in their emotions.

The crocuses are a sign of spring and new life, and Catherine is pleased to see them when her fever is better, because they remind her of the Heights. Still, she knows she will never see them or the moors again.

45

What is happening to Isabella?

? Has your opinion about Isabella's character changed in any way?

? In what way do you think she is being influenced by the atmosphere at Wuthering Heights?

find out more about Isabella's marriage from hell – after the break

CHAPTER 14

◆ March 1784: Edgar is still unforgiving of Isabella
◆ Nelly visits the Heights; she is shocked by the state of the place
◆ Isabella is being dragged down to its level; only Heathcliff looks good
◆ Nelly lectures Isabella about her foolishness; Heathcliff insists on seeing Catherine
◆ He compares the depth of his love for Catherine with Edgar's
◆ Heathcliff describes Isabella's love for him; he suggests that she enjoys cruelty
◆ He threatens to imprison Nelly if she stops him from seeing Catherine
◆ Nelly promises to take a letter to Catherine from him
◆ The narration returns to Lockwood, who thinks about his attraction to Cathy and worries that she may have turned out like her mother

In this chapter, Nelly reports on the state of the Heights and its inhabitants. Heathcliff seems to infect everyone there with his hatred and brutality. Isabella is so paralyzed by the atmosphere that she cannot even keep herself clean. We also see the moralistic side of Nelly when she blames Isabella for her predicament; yet Nelly is shocked by Heathcliff's sadistic behavior toward his wife. What is strange is that Isabella seems to come to life. It seems as if she can feel emotion only when he is acting badly toward her.

The chapter is also important in the way it lets us see Heathcliff's moral code. He despises Edgar's morality with its ordinary *duty* and *humanity*. He believes Catherine and he are above such petty, everyday rules. We also see Heathcliff's obsessive desire for revenge when he exclaims *the more the worms writhe, the more I yearn to crush out their entrails.*

Nelly is torn between loyalty to Edgar and fear of what Heathcliff might do, so she agrees to take a letter to Catherine.

The narration returns to Lockwood, who mentions his attraction to Cathy. There is a feeling of history repeating itself when he speaks of her *brilliant eyes*, and worries that she might turn out like her mother.

 STYLE AND LANGUAGE

Brontë uses a series of vivid similes and **metaphors** to describe the nature of Heathcliff's love for Catherine. *Catherine has a heart as deep as I have; the sea could be as readily contained in that horse-trough, as her whole affection be monopolized by him.* He uses "horse-trough" to pour scorn on Edgar's earthly, limited love. It acts as a contrast with the power and magnificence of the sea, which is like the love Heathcliff and Catherine share. He believes that Catherine is *in hell* being surrounded by people who cannot feel like herself and Heathcliff. They *might as well plant an oak in a flower pot, and expect it to thrive.* This metaphor contrasts Catherine's untamed, passionate nature with Edgar's calmer, more domestic love.

Isabella is forced upstairs by Heathcliff. Nelly is threatened with imprisonment at the Heights if she does not take a letter to Catherine. This is an earlier version of what happens to Cathy and herself later in the novel.

The mystery of Heathcliff

? Heathcliff's behavior goes from bad to worse. Add examples of his actions to your Heathcliff Mini Mind Map. Remember to use key word quotations.

Heathcliff and Catherine have a passionate meeting – find out more after your break

CHAPTER 15

- January 1802: Lockwood's narration opens the chapter
- Nelly takes up the story; March 19, 1784: Catherine is still very weak
- She reads the letter, then Heathcliff enters and realizes she is dying
- An emotional scene between them; Catherine faints
- Edgar returns; he tries to bring Catherine around, but she is in a deep faint
- Heathcliff will not leave the garden, so he can be near her

Another important chapter, in which Heathcliff's passionate speech shows the terrible result of Catherine's decision to marry Edgar. Once full of life and energy, Catherine now seems almost ghostlike in her white gown and pale, haggard face. Her manner is dreamy, her gaze *out of this world*. All these descriptions emphasize that she is near death. Only Heathcliff has the power to temporarily lift her out of this state. We see the strength of their passion, physical as well as emotional, as she pulls out a lock of Heathcliff's hair during their embrace, while he leaves bruises on her arm from holding her too tightly.

In his agony, Heathcliff accuses her of betraying her own heart. Brontë seems to be suggesting that Catherine is dying because she went against her natural instincts by marrying Edgar. ❂Do you agree with this point of view? Could Catherine and Heathcliff have had a happy marriage? What is so unbearable for Heathcliff is the thought that he will have to stay alive when she is dead, but with his *soul in the grave*. This is the key to Heathcliff's emotional state throughout the rest of the novel. He is tortured by loss and cannot live a complete life without Catherine.

Nelly seems cool and distant from all this emotion, so much so that when Catherine faints, she thinks *far better that she should be dead, than lingering a burden and a misery-maker to all about her.* ❸What do you think about Nelly's reactions?

There are numerous references to death in this chapter, from Catherine's appearance to the mention of graves. It is clear that she welcomes death. Hell and devils and "things infernal" are also mentioned. Heathcliff is always described in these terms anyway, and their relationship is so wild and passionate it would be difficult to associate it with heaven.

Catherine always sits beside the open window. She likes to look across to the moors. It is as if her soul, as well as her body, wants freedom now, and the mention of windows emphasizes this.

CHAPTER 16

- ◆ March 19–20, 1784: Cathy is born at midnight; Catherine dies
- ◆ Edgar is left without a male heir
- ◆ Nelly breaks the news to Heathcliff; he curses Catherine for leaving him
- ◆ Catherine is buried in the churchyard on the moor

The contrast between Edgar's grief and that of Heathcliff is typical of them. Edgar is still and quiet and looks as if he himself has died, whereas Heathcliff has been wounding himself against the tree in his violent sorrow. He is once again compared to an animal when he howls *like a savage beast.*

Cathy's birth is overshadowed by Catherine's death. Nelly also looks at the baby and remembers that Edgar's father left the property to Isabella, not Edgar. She is worried about Heathcliff inheriting the family fortunes through his wife.

Heathcliff makes sure it is his lock of hair joined with Catherine's in the locket. He throws Edgar's lock away, as if her husband has no right to be connected to her.

The author uses repetition or echo again. Cathy's entry into life is as contradictory and sorrowful as Hareton's. In each case, the joy of a new baby is linked with the death of the mother. Heathcliff is soaked with dew. It is as if nature is also crying for the death of Catherine.

CHAPTER 17

- ◆ March 25, 1784: Isabella runs away; she arrives at the Grange
- ◆ She tells Nelly about her terrible life with Heathcliff
- ◆ Violence at the Heights is brought to a crisis point by Catherine's death
- ◆ Hindley locks Heathcliff out
- ◆ Hindley's plan to kill Heathcliff backfires, and he is shot and stabbed with his own weapons
- ◆ Heathcliff attacks the unconscious Hindley, but stops and binds his wounds
- ◆ Isabella tells Hindley of the attack the next day
- ◆ She provokes Heathcliff into violence toward her, then escapes
- ◆ She moves to the south and bears a son
- ◆ Edgar's depression lifts and he forms a strong bond with little Cathy
- ◆ September 1784: Hindley dies; Nelly is suspicious
- ◆ Heathcliff inherits the Heights, Hareton is robbed of his inheritance

This chapter contains further scenes of violence. Even Isabella's choice of words shows how she has been affected. She calls Heathcliff an *incarnate goblin* and describes her attempts to exasperate him as *pulling out the nerves with red hot pincers.*

Isabella seems half mad when she arrives at the Grange and doesn't care that the house is in mourning for Catherine. She destroys her wedding ring, then describes the incredible events she has seen. Hindley tries to kill Heathcliff but, instead, is almost murdered himself. Heathcliff's violent nature is emphasized when Isabella describes his sharp teeth.

Isabella has been so hardened by her experiences that she feels no sympathy for Heathcliff's grief over Catherine. Indeed, she hardly seems surprised to see Hareton hanging a litter of puppies. No one escapes the poison of brutality in this household, even a young child.

Heathcliff hears that Isabella has given birth to their child and makes it clear that he will take *it* when the time suits him. ❍Why does he refer to his son as "it"?

Despite these terrible events, there is new life and hope at the Grange because of the baby, Cathy. There is contrast between her upbringing and the way Heathcliff promises to bring up Hareton. *We'll see if one tree won't grow as crooked as another, with the same wind to twist it!* ●Who are the two trees? What does Heathcliff intend to do?

Brontë does not always describe a pleasant view of childhood. This chapter shows how children's happiness depends on the adults who raise them. Heathcliff was damaged by his upbringing and is now doing worse to Hareton. Even the newborn Cathy is described as a *moaning doll*, and is unwanted at first.

Isabella reads because she is bored and unhappy, not from real choice.

The weather is used as a background to the sorrow of the household at the Grange. Although the weather was fair for Catherine's funeral, the household is now in mourning and there is an atmosphere of sad emptiness. *The larks were silent, the young leaves ... smitten and blackened.*

Life at Wuthering Heights goes from bad to worse. Heathcliff degrades both Hindley and Hareton. Isabella escapes from her brutal marriage and describes the horrors she has seen there. Heathcliff and Catherine meet for the last time. Cathy is born; Catherine dies.

Section 5 Chapters 18–20

CHAPTER 18

- 1797: 12 happy years pass
- Cathy, 13 years old, is sheltered by her father
- Edgar leaves to visit the dying Isabella
- Cathy runs off one day; she ends up at the Heights
- Contrast between her and Hareton
- Hareton is now a young man with no manners or social skills

This chapter adds to the sense of a fairy tale that runs through the novel. Cathy is like a young princess who can no longer be protected from the bad spell (Heathcliff). Edgar tries to shield his daughter from the outside world, but it is easy to predict that she will eventually break loose. Her need for freedom reminds the reader of her mother, Catherine, and goes along with the novel's idea of life being a cycle or wheel. It does not just repeat itself, however. ❶Do you think Cathy will have a better chance of happiness than her mother? What parts of the chapter suggest this to you?

We also see the effects of upbringing once again. Hareton is born into the same class as Cathy, but she is brought up as a young lady, whereas he is described as *good things lost amid a wilderness of weeds.* Joseph adds to Hareton's degradation by encouraging the boy's bad manners and behavior. ❶Remind yourself of Heathcliff as a young boy and compare the descriptions of him with those of Hareton.

Brontë uses the image of a field or garden to describe Hareton's character and his potential. *Evidence of a wealthy soil that might yield luxuriant crops.*

Cathy refuses to believe that Hareton is her cousin because he is uneducated, poorly dressed, and speaks with a local accent. Instead, she treats him like a servant.

Cathy is now at the age where she cannot be protected from the world and wants more freedom.

Mother and daughter

? Look back at your character notes or Mind Map on Catherine. Now begin adding details about Cathy. Try to build up a picture of their similarities and differences.

Cathy gets a new playmate, just like her mother before her – but Linton isn't a chip off the old block. Find out why after your break

CHAPTER 19

- ◆ June 1797: Isabella dies
- ◆ Young Linton is to arrive; Cathy is delighted
- ◆ Linton is sickly and weak
- ◆ Joseph arrives to bring the boy to Heathcliff

Cathy is excited at the thought of a playmate, but when Linton arrives it is clear that he is weak and tearful, unlike his healthy cousin, Hareton. He is made to sound very young compared to Cathy, even though there is only six months' age difference.

Joseph enjoys doing Heathcliff's unpleasant work for him. We get a sense of children's lack of rights at this time. Linton is treated like another piece of Heathcliff's property.

CHAPTER 20

- ◆ Linton is moved to the Heights early the next day
- ◆ Heathcliff gives his son a harsh welcome
- ◆ Heathcliff reassures Nelly that Linton will be looked after properly, as he wants the boy's money

Linton is unwilling to go to the Heights, so Nelly reassures him that *all children love their parents.* ◑Why is this **ironic**?

Linton does not get a good impression of his future life at the Heights, as the outside of the house looks unwelcoming and uncared for. Heathcliff makes fun of the child's pale and sickly looks. More important, he explains his plan of revenge. *I want the triumph of seeing **my** descendant fairly lord of their estates; my child hiring their children, to till their father's lands for wages.* He intends to take the lands from the Lintons and Earnshaws, then make their descendants work for Linton and his descendants.

The idea of repetition or a cycle occurs again in the description of Linton, who resembles Isabella and the fair-haired Linton family.

The new generation is growing up. Cathy is happy and well adjusted; Hareton is uneducated and degraded; Linton is attractive, but weak and in poor health.

Section 6 Chapters 21–28

CHAPTER 21

- ◆ Cathy is distressed about Linton's departure
- ◆ Zillah speaks to Nelly about Linton's poor health and selfish ways
- ◆ Three years pass: March 1800—Cathy's 16th birthday
- ◆ She and Nelly meet Heathcliff on the moors; he persuades them to visit the Heights
- ◆ Heathcliff tells Nelly that he wants Linton and Cathy to be married
- ◆ Heathcliff alters the truth about the quarrel between himself and Linton
- ◆ Cathy and Linton plan future visits
- ◆ Contrast between Hareton and Linton
- ◆ Cathy makes fun of Hareton because he cannot read
- ◆ Edgar tries to convince her of Heathcliff's bad nature, but she is torn about breaking her promise to Linton
- ◆ Nelly finds a pile of letters from Linton to Cathy; she forbids her to write again

The links between the generations continue with this chapter. The three young people meet now that they have grown. Brontë sets this chapter on Cathy's 16th birthday, which is also the anniversary of her mother's death. This is significant, because her relationship with Linton begins, marking the end of one period in her life and the beginning of another. Nelly hints at trouble to come. She describes the perfect day, then adds *it's a pity she could not be content*. When Cathy runs ahead, Nelly cannot keep up, which is a sign that the young woman is beginning to break free from the control of her father and nurse.

Heathcliff wants Linton to marry Cathy. Because old Mr. Linton left everything to Isabella and not Edgar, young Linton is the heir. ✪What is Heathcliff trying to do here? How will this marriage help him to get further revenge on the two families?

Although Heathcliff has deliberately degraded Hareton, he would have preferred Hareton for his son. Hareton is strong, handsome, and straightforward. Ironically, he adores Heathcliff, even though his life has been ruined by him.

Like her mother's and Edgar's attraction, Cathy is attracted to the fair, slender Linton, yet the pair are strikingly different. ❍Why does Cathy go along with Linton when he mocks Hareton for his ignorance?

Heathcliff can barely hide his contempt for Linton, and calls him *it* again. We also see how Heathcliff has shaped Hareton. ❍Who is Hareton compared to? Why is Heathcliff's enjoyment in ruining Hareton so very cruel? (*I've pleasure in him.*) Young Linton's weakness of health and character make him very different from his father. He seems to have inherited the worst qualities of young Isabella and Edgar. Zillah gives a description of Linton's selfish behavior and later, his mockery of Hareton. Brontë is preparing us for Linton's betrayal of Cathy later in the story.

Cathy learns about Heathcliff's cruelty when Edgar tells her about Isabella's disastrous marriage. Cathy has been sheltered from the world and the story shocks her. Although she understands why she should stay away from Heathcliff, she feels great conflict about not seeing Linton. Her kind side is revealed when Nelly finds her crying about having to disappoint Linton and break her promise. It is this that makes her disobey her father and write to the boy. ❍Do you think Cathy is as willful as her mother? What is different about the two characters?

The gap between Hareton, and Linton and Cathy is shown mainly by Hareton's inability to read. They humiliate him for this and also for his broad Yorkshire accent.

Linton prefers to be indoors and in bed to being outside with nature. Beds are often described in a similar way to coffins or graves in the novel, so this shows how close the boy is to death.

 ## STYLE AND LANGUAGE

Windows and doors are used to show the difference between Cathy and Linton. He always prefers staying indoors to going outside, unlike Cathy who loves the freedom of the moors. He insists on having the windows closed, while she looks at the door with *longing*.

One is gold put to the use of paving-stones; and the other is tin polished to ape a service of silver. Heathcliff is talking about Linton and Hareton here. ❂Which description fits which boy? What do the two metaphors mean?

The generation game

?   Look at the descriptions of Cathy and Linton. Compare these with your Mind Maps on Catherine and Edgar.

?   Make a Mind Map showing similarities and differences.

?   Make key word notes about their characters, as well as physical appearance.

will Heathcliff get his evil way? Find out about a budding romance after the break

CHAPTER 22

◆ Edgar is ill; Cathy is depressed
◆ While out walking, they meet Heathcliff
◆ He tells Cathy off for disappointing Linton and says the boy is sick with misery
◆ Cathy is determined to see Linton

Cathy feels depressed because she cannot see Linton. She is also sad because her father is ill. She expresses her fears about being left all alone. Nelly comforts her but also gives her a stern warning about disobeying her father, saying that this will put his health at risk.

We see the young woman's determination and growing maturity when she says that she must visit Linton, to make sure that Heathcliff is lying. She realizes that she cannot trust

Heathcliff or just accept what Nelly says and must make up her own mind.

 OHow does the weather act as a background to Cathy's mood in this chapter?

CHAPTER 23

- ◆ Cathy and Nelly arrive at the Heights
- ◆ Linton is ill, neglected, and bad-tempered
- ◆ Cathy and Linton discuss marriage, then quarrel about their families
- ◆ She pushes his chair in anger and he has a bad coughing fit
- ◆ They make up; she mothers him
- ◆ Nelly is furious that Cathy intends to visit Linton again
- ◆ Nelly is ill; Cathy looks after her and Edgar
- ◆ Cathy secretly visits the Heights at night

Joseph is his usual unpleasant self and neglecting Linton, who is very ill. Although Nelly is irritated by the boy's miserable and complaining nature, it is clear that he is genuinely ill. He uses his illness to get attention, but is genuinely unloved and uncared for. **O**Cathy is more sympathetic than Nelly toward Linton. Whose side are you on, and why?

The hatred between Heathcliff and the Lintons is brought into the open when Cathy and Linton argue about their parents' relationships. In this way, it can be seen how the acts of the previous generation affect the children, even though they were not even born when the tragedies took place.

Cathy can be hot tempered like her mother, but she also has a kind heart, as when she does her best to calm Linton. She does not bear grudges, whereas Linton milks the situation for as long as he can. Their relationship is more like brother and sister or mother and child than future husband and wife.

Nelly tries to talk Cathy out of her feelings for Linton by telling her that he will not live long. **O**Do you think she is wise to do this? Why?

Cathy shows her growing independence in two ways. First, she declares *The Grange is not my prison, Ellen, and you are not my jailer;* then she visits the Heights, despite being forbidden to do so. Cathy now has to take more responsibility for the family by looking after Nelly and her father, but she is also determined to have more of a life for herself.

Real love

? Find examples of the way Linton treats Cathy as a mother figure. Underline the quotations and make notes in your copy of the novel if permitted, or write it up in your Mind Maps.

Hareton tries to better himself, but is mocked. Linton and Cathy quarrel. Find out how – after the break

CHAPTER 24

- ◆ 1800: Nelly discovers that Cathy has been visiting the Heights
- ◆ Cathy becomes the narrator
- ◆ She tells Nelly about her visits
- ◆ Cathy and Linton's idea of a perfect day
- ◆ Hareton has taught himself to read, but Cathy makes fun of him
- ◆ He is angry and throws Linton and Cathy out of the kitchen
- ◆ Linton is very angry and has a coughing fit
- ◆ He blames Cathy for the incident when she returns
- ◆ She forgives him and they make up; she learns to accept his behavior
- ◆ November 1800: the narration returns to Nelly, who tells Edgar everything; he stops the visits

The shift between Nelly and Cathy as narrators in the last two chapters shows us another side to Linton. Brontë lets Cathy speak, and we see her describing her relationship with the boy from her point of view. It is also a sign that the young woman is making her own decisions, rightly or wrongly.

Cathy makes fun of Hareton's attempts to educate himself. This is thoughtless and cruel. He wants her approval and is so angry when she taunts him that he throws Cathy and Linton out of the kitchen. ❂What do you think Hareton feels about their relationship?

Linton's rage at this is like a weak version of Heathcliff's, and typically, Joseph enjoys seeing the boy angry and powerless. It is also typical of Linton that he rejects Cathy, the one person who really cares about him. It is only Cathy's affection and concern that make her return and make up after their quarrel. Linton shows a rare moment of honesty when he apologizes. He loves her and dislikes himself, but cannot improve his behavior. Cathy is realistic about his nature, but very loyal to him, because she realizes he has no one else.

✒ STYLE AND LANGUAGE

Cathy has continued the visits to Linton, even though he has often behaved badly toward her. The quarrel they have about heaven tells the reader a lot about them. Cathy's heaven is full of wind, light, and movement, *the whole world awake and wild with joy.* Linton just wants to lie still all day in the sun. It is rather like his desire to stay in bed and not take part in life, whereas Cathy's heaven shows her energy and enjoyment of all living things.

 Linton and Cathy share a love of books. Hareton wants to be included in this world so he tries to teach himself to read. Cathy also uses books to bribe a servant so she can visit the Heights.

CHAPTER 25

- ◆ 1802: the narration returns to Nelly
- ◆ She teases Lockwood about his fascination with Cathy, then returns to the story
- ◆ Summer 1801: Edgar is close to death; he confides in Nelly about his fears for Cathy; Linton writes a letter asking to meet Edgar; Nelly suspects some of it was written by

Heathcliff
- Edgar agrees to let the pair meet on the moors
- No one realizes how ill Linton is

Nelly teases Lockwood about his interest in Cathy but he refuses to do anything about the young woman. ❍How does this remind you of Lockwood's actions in the first chapters of the novel?

Edgar is dying, and worries about Cathy being left alone when he is gone. He does not care about Heathcliff getting his own way, but is concerned that Linton will be too weak to protect Cathy from Heathcliff's *wickedness*. After Linton's letters and Cathy's pleading, he allows them to meet on the moors. No one realizes that the boy is dying and that Heathcliff is *avaricious* (greedy) and *unfeeling* by forcing him to ride and walk with Cathy. Nelly does not realize this until later, of course, so her comments are made in hindsight (knowledge obtained after the event).

Edgar always visits his wife's grave on Cathy's birthday, but this time he does not. It seems as if he is so close to death that he knows he will be reunited with her soon. Linton is also dying.

Brontë's use of two dying characters, as well as the pattern of very short chapters at this point of the novel, adds to the sense of events moving quickly.

CHAPTER 26

- August 1801: Nelly accompanies Cathy to meet Linton
- He looks ill and weak, but calms Cathy's fears, although Nelly is alarmed
- He seems frightened of his father

Linton is very different, and Cathy cannot understand it, although Nelly fears the worst. She is direct and asks him if Heathcliff has started beating him.

Cathy is naïve about Linton's poor health, just as she does not understand that Edgar is dying. She is disappointed in Linton, who is too ill to respond to her, but begins to worry about him on the way home.

Ironically, the "heavenly" summer's day once described by Linton as perfect, is here, but he is too ill to enjoy it.

CHAPTER 27

- August 1801: Edgar is fading fast; he hopes Cathy will be happy when she is married to Linton
- Cathy and Nelly meet with Linton again
- He is weaker than ever, paralyzed by fear
- Cathy is unsympathetic at first
- Heathcliff arrives and threatens the boy
- Cathy is forced to go to the Heights to protect Linton
- Heathcliff locks them in
- Cathy stands up to him, but he beats her
- Heathcliff plans to force them to marry
- Nelly is locked up alone for days

The beautiful August weather seems to give hope and life, yet is tinged with sadness because Edgar is dying. It also provides a strong contrast to Heathcliff's cruelty and violence. Linton's fear is so strong and Nelly is so puzzled by it that it seems almost supernatural. Linton is *powerless* against it.

Cathy's behavior toward Heathcliff lets the reader see why she became the angry, bitter person that Lockwood met at the beginning of the novel. Despite her courage, he beats her. Heathcliff is made even angrier by the resemblance to her mother.

Nelly does not understand Cathy's willingness to marry Linton. ❂Why does Cathy want to marry Linton? Is it just so she can be with her dying father?

✒ STYLE AND LANGUAGE

The language in this chapter becomes more urgent and desperate, as Linton tries to avoid Heathcliff's violence, Nelly and Cathy try to escape from the Heights, and Heathcliff makes sure the pair is married before Linton dies.

 Heathcliff keeps the two women prisoner, and has also threatened to lock his sick son out of his home. Cathy is physically and emotionally trapped by the situation because her father is near death. The windows are too narrow to let them escape. Cathy's mood matches the changing light on the moors.

Wordpower

? Make a list of words or phrases in this chapter that describe fear or anger, for example, distraught, trembled, snatched, struck, curbed ferocity.

dire deeds and death. Find out about Heathcliff's villainy after the break

CHAPTER 28

- ◆ Nelly is released by Zillah, the housekeeper
- ◆ Linton will not help her to release Cathy
- ◆ Nelly returns to the Grange
- ◆ Edgar intends to alter his will so that Heathcliff cannot inherit when Linton dies
- ◆ September 1801: Cathy escapes; she is with her father when he dies
- ◆ Heathcliff has bribed the lawyer, so Edgar cannot change the will

Nelly reminds Linton about Cathy's kindness to him. His conscience is not moved; all he is interested in is her money. The word "marriage" is never mentioned, but he speaks of owning everything that once belonged to Cathy so it is clear that the wedding has taken place. This is an echo of his father's own loveless marriage to Isabella.

❍Why does Heathcliff destroy the portrait of Edgar from Catherine's locket? Who was in the other portrait? The separation of the two portraits is a symbol – of what?

Cathy escapes through her mother's bedroom window by the fir tree, and her return to the Grange is marked by a soft, persistent knocking. These details are another example of the novel's circular form, because they are a reminder of her mother's ghost trying to get into Lockwood's window at the beginning of the novel.

Three years pass. The new generation meets again. Secret letters and visits between Cathy and Linton. Hareton and Cathy clash, as do Linton and Hareton. Echoes of the generation before them. Linton very ill, Edgar also. Heathcliff kidnaps Cathy, forces her into marriage. Linton gets the family money and Edgar dies without being able to change his will in Cathy's favor—the next step of Heathcliff's revenge is achieved.

Section 7 Chapters 29–34

CHAPTER 29

- ◆ September 1801: Thrushcross Grange now Heathcliff's; he walks in to claim it
- ◆ Linton has been punished; he is mad with fear of Heathcliff
- ◆ Cathy is forced to go the Heights and take care of him
- ◆ Heathcliff describes Linton's vicious nature
- ◆ Cathy still loves Linton; she expresses her pity for Heathcliff
- ◆ Heathcliff tells Nelly about looking at Catherine in her coffin
- ◆ He has had coffins changed so that he can lie next to her

◆ When Catherine was first buried, he tried to dig up her body, but felt her spirit near him and was comforted

◆ Since then, she has come and gone; he has lived in torture

◆ He takes Cathy back to the Heights; Nelly is forbidden to visit

Edgar has only just been buried when Heathcliff comes to claim his inheritance. Heathcliff is without pity, as can be seen by the way he enjoys Linton's fear of him. Cathy's pity for the lonely, miserable Heathcliff is spoken in *dreary triumph*. Already, the loveless atmosphere of the Heights is affecting her.

Heathcliff's macabre description about looking at Catherine in the grave shocks the reader and makes us realize just how obsessed Heathcliff is about being reunited with his love. There are hints that he will be a wandering ghost if he is not buried next to Catherine. ❂Why does he speak of *sleep* rather than death?

We learn that this is not the first time he has tried to get at the buried Catherine; he tried to dig her up when she first died. He describes the past 18 years as torture. Catherine has been as unpredictable in death as she was in life, sometimes visiting him in spirit form, but leaving him alone most of the time. ❂What are your feelings toward Heathcliff at this point?

Death and sleep are described in almost similar ways. Perhaps this is a sign that Heathcliff sees death as a welcome rest from his unhappy life. It also suggests that he believes in some sort of afterlife with Catherine. Graves and beds are described in a similar way; for example, when Heathcliff tries to sleep in Catherine's old room, her spirit stays with him, even lying on the pillow. The reader does not have to believe in ghosts. What is important is that Heathcliff is convinced of Catherine's presence, and has been affected by this belief for half of his life.

CHAPTER 30

◆ Zillah gives Nelly news; Cathy is unhappy and disliked by everyone

- Linton is ill; Heathcliff refuses to get the doctor; Zillah will not help Cathy
- October 1801: Linton dies; Cathy is all alone and penniless; she stays upstairs for two weeks
- She comes downstairs one Sunday; she rejects Zillah's and Hareton's help
- She allows Hareton to bring books to her
- He strokes her hair; she is angry with him
- Cathy cuts herself off from anyone's help; she grows more bitter and bad tempered
- January 1802: Nelly finishes her narration; Lockwood announces that he is leaving for London

Linton dies, with only Cathy to mourn him. She also feels *like death*, and locks herself away. Her return to the household is like returning to life, even if it is miserable and unwelcoming. She cannot bear to stay in the freezing upstairs room, but the cold is also emotional. It is as if her unhappiness has frozen her spirit. She says she has been *starved,* a Yorkshire term for cold, but this is a reminder of her mother's refusal to eat at the beginning of her illness. ❂There is a similarity between the way mother and daughter react to extreme unhappiness. Can you see a difference between them also?

Another reminder about the circular style of the novel is the way the uncouth Hareton is so similar to the young Heathcliff. Both are embarrassed by the presence of a beautiful and educated young woman and try to clean themselves up. Cathy is proud like her mother.

It is significant that when Cathy returns to the household and gets warm, she immediately turns to books. Perhaps this is a sign that she is taking some pleasure in life again. Hareton helps her to reach the books, and wants her to read to him. Although she rejects him, he is beginning to share in the world of books.

CHAPTER 31

- Lockwood takes Nelly's message to the Heights
- Cathy rejects the letter; Hareton lets her have it back

- ◆ Heathcliff has destroyed her books
- ◆ Hareton is embarrassed when Cathy says she has found his hidden books
- ◆ He gives them to her, despite her rudeness
- ◆ She continues to humiliate him about his poor reading skills
- ◆ He throws the books into the fire, even though he does not want to lose them
- ◆ Lockwood guesses Hareton's reasons for wanting to read
- ◆ Heathcliff returns; he looks *restless* and *anxious*
- ◆ Lockwood is invited for dinner

Lockwood is uncomfortable at the quarreling between Hareton and Cathy. Cathy has grown more spiteful because of her unhappiness. Lockwood realizes that Hareton wants to be accepted by Cathy, which is why he is trying to read. She is angry at the way he reads her favorite books so badly and continues to provoke him. He burns the books, even though they have brought him so much pleasure.

Heathcliff comments on the growing resemblance between Cathy and Hareton. ❂What has happened to Hareton to make the resemblance more obvious? We also get an idea that Heathcliff feels affection for Hareton, for he mutters *it will be odd, if I thwart myself.* Heathcliff worries that he will spoil his revenge by helping Hareton.

Books are Cathy's link with a better, happier life, which is why Heathcliff destroys them. Hareton wants to be part of this because he is attracted to her. He also gets pleasure from words and ideas, because his natural intelligence has been starved for so long.

CHAPTER 32

- ◆ September 1802: Lockwood is back in the neighborhood
- ◆ Nelly is no longer the housekeeper at the Grange
- ◆ Lockwood visits the Heights
- ◆ The place is welcoming and homelike
- ◆ He sees Hareton and Cathy reading together
- ◆ Nelly is singing; Joseph is complaining

- She returns to her narration
- January 1802: Nelly returns to the Heights to take care of Cathy
- Easter 1802: the beginnings of friendship between Cathy and Hareton

Wuthering Heights is changed, and so is the behavior of its inhabitants. Things are so different that Lockwood describes Hareton and Cathy without mentioning their names. ❖What is the effect of this on the reader, do you think?

Another important sign of change is in the behavior of Nelly and Joseph. He is still twisted and speaks of Hareton being "witched" by Cathy, but he has lost his power to hurt now. Nelly sings happily and just laughs at him. She is also warm and welcoming toward Lockwood.

Nelly brings Lockwood up to date. When she returns to the Heights in January, Cathy has become more bitter and quarrelsome, but there are important signs of change when she tries to heal the divisions between herself and Hareton. Cathy is a little like a princess in a fairy tale here, because her kiss transforms him. *He trembled and his face glowed – all his rudeness, and all his surly harshness had deserted him.*

The window and door symbolism is used here to show the change in Cathy's life. At the beginning of the chapter, the windows and doors are open, but when the story moves back in time, Cathy is still a prisoner, sitting by the window but unable to go outside.

Cathy gives Hareton the present of a book and puts his name on the package. It is a sign that she now wants to welcome him into the world of books and have him as a friend.

Same house, different lives

?   Can you see the difference in the appearance of the house in Chapter 32, compared to its description in Chapters 1 and 2?

?   How do the changes in the house fit in with the changes in the lives of the characters?

? Make a Mini Mind Map to show the contrasts, using key words.

who dug up the currant bushes? Take a break before finding out

CHAPTER 33

◆ March 1802: Cathy and Hareton move Joseph's currant bushes to make a flower bed
◆ Heathcliff tells Cathy off
◆ She accuses him of having stolen wealth from herself and Hareton
◆ Heathcliff threatens to throw Hareton out if she continues to influence him
◆ Hareton refuses to believe anything bad about Heathcliff
◆ Heathcliff notices the resemblance of Cathy and Hareton to Catherine
◆ He describes his feelings about the two young people
◆ He has lost the urge for revenge, and also his will to live

The removal of Joseph's fruit bushes is a sign that change is coming to Wuthering Heights. The young lovers want to change the prickly bushes for a beautiful bed of flowers. This is a sign that they are taking control of their home, and also that the harshness of Heathcliff's and Joseph's rule is coming to an end. Another example of the change is Cathy's playfulness when she puts primroses in Hareton's porridge. Heathcliff cannot stand their happiness. She also confronts Heathcliff about the inheritance for the first time.

Heathcliff's anger with Cathy is frightening, but his mood changes and he looks at her intently. ❍Why do you think he changes his mind about hitting her?

Hareton is loyal to Heathcliff. ❍Do you think he is right? How does Hareton's behavior show the difference between the two generations?

Heathcliff's conversation with Nelly shows that the past is catching up with him. He is haunted by Catherine. Not only do Cathy and Hareton remind him of her, but everything does. *The entire world is a dreadful collection of memoranda that she did exist, and that I have lost her!* He longs for death.

CHAPTER 34

◆ April 1802: Heathcliff avoids everyone
◆ He returns one day; his behavior is *wild and glad*
◆ He stops eating
◆ Nelly is frightened by his appearance one evening
◆ She dreams about him
◆ He continues to refuse food; he sees things that nobody else can see
◆ Nelly tries to persuade him to see a minister; he is not interested in Christian ideas of heaven
◆ May 1802: He goes to his room and refuses to come out; Nelly finds him dead
◆ Hareton grieves for him
◆ Local people say Heathcliff's ghost walks
◆ Lockwood leaves, avoiding the young lovers
◆ He visits the three graves; he does not believe in the ghost stories

It is spring at the Heights, a time of new life and hope. Hareton and Cathy work on the garden, a symbol of their new life together. Heathcliff, on the other hand, avoids company and stops eating, a sign that he is ending his life. His behavior becomes unpredictable and strange, but he is not violent or angry. The way his happiness is described makes him seem unnatural and frightening.

Everything associated with Heathcliff's illness and death is described in a supernatural way: *The light flashed on his features ... left me in darkness.* ❂Why does Nelly think such things? Do you think she is just superstitious?

This theme is continued when Heathcliff sees things invisible to others. In death, his face has a *life-like gaze of exultation*

(triumph, joy). ✪What do you think he saw as he died?
Although Nelly says she does not believe in the local tales
about the ghosts of Heathcliff and Catherine, she does mention
her meeting with the frightened young shepherd who has seen
something. Only Lockwood is skeptical (unbelieving).
However, he runs away from Hareton and Cathy to avoid seeing
them, just as he did in Chapter 32. He brings his loneliness on
himself, but cannot bear to see the happiness of others. He won't
believe that the dead lovers are restless in their graves. ✪Do you
think he is the kind of man who understands such a powerful
love? What is your opinion about whether the souls of Heathcliff
and Catherine rest in peace or not?

Heathcliff inherits everything. Linton dies and Cathy is depressed. The
relationship between Hareton and Cathy develops. Heathcliff loses the will to
live, and dies. Love and decency return to Wuthering Heights in the form of
Cathy and Hareton's impending marriage.

*now that you've finished going through the
text, take a well-earned break*

TOPICS FOR DISCUSSION AND BRAINSTORMING

One of the best ways to review is with one or more friends. Even if you're with someone who hardly knows the text you're studying, you'll find that having to explain things to your friend will help you to organize your own thoughts and memorize key points. If you're with someone who has studied the text, you'll find that the things you can't remember are different from the things your friend can't remember, so you'll be able to help each other.

Discussion will also help you to develop interesting new ideas that perhaps neither of you would have had alone. Use a **brainstorming** approach to tackle any of the topics listed on the following page. Allow yourself to share whatever ideas come into your head, however meaningless they seem. This will get you thinking creatively.

Whether alone or with a friend, use Mind Mapping (see p. vii) to help you brainstorm and organize your ideas. If you are with a friend, use a large sheet of paper and colored pens.

Any of the topics on the following page could appear on an exam, but even if you think you've found one on your actual exam, be sure to answer the precise question given.

TOPICS

1 Discuss the idea of love and marriage in the novel. Make a Mind Map of the characters who marry. Decide on the good and bad points of each marriage.

2 Heathcliff is a monster and the reader cannot feel any sympathy for him. Discuss this idea, then MOG (**M**ind Map, **O**rganize, **G**ather).

3 Why does Emily Brontë use flashbacks in the novel? Look particularly at the last four or five chapters.

4 What's in a name? Do a brainstorm for each name in the story; for example, how does Heathcliff's name fit with what you know about his character?

5 Make a Mind Map about the theme of "books" in the novel. Show the ways in which books are used by different characters for good and bad purposes; for example, Edgar Linton reads to escape from the problems in his relationship with Catherine (bad), whereas Hareton reads because his mind has been starved of ideas and beautiful things (good).

6 Write a short character study comparing Catherine and Cathy.

7 With a friend, role-play Heathcliff being interviewed by a local newspaper reporter after Linton's death. Get your partner to ask you questions about how you obtained your money. Imagine the angry replies Heathcliff would make!

HOW TO GET AN "A" IN ENGLISH LITERATURE

In all your study, in coursework, and in exams, be aware of the following:

- **Characterization** – the characters and how we know about them (what they say and do, how the author describes them), their relationships, and how they develop.
- **Plot and structure** – what happens and how the plot is organized into parts or episodes.
- **Setting and atmosphere** – the changing scene and how it reflects the story (for example, a rugged landscape and storm reflecting a character's emotional difficulties). This is called "pathetic fallacy."
- **Viewpoint** – how the story is told (for example, through an imaginary narrator, or in the third person, or through a series of different narrators).
- **Social and historical context** – influences on the author (see Background in this guide).

Develop your ability to:

- Relate **detail** to **broader content, meaning, and style**.
- Show understanding of the author's **intentions, technique, and meaning** (brief and appropriate comparisons with other works by the same author will earn credit).
- Give a **personal response and interpretation**, backed up by **examples** and short **quotations**.
- **Evaluate** the author's achievement (how far does the author succeed and why?).

Make sure you:

- Know how to use **paragraphs** correctly.
- Use a wide range of vocabulary and sentence structure.
- Use short, appropriate quotations as **evidence** of your understanding of that part of the text.

- Answer the question, don't just tell the story. Your teacher and the examiner know it already; you've got to show that you can apply your understanding to one particular part of the novel, such as a theme or a character.
- Use literary terms to show your understanding of what the author is trying to achieve with language. Some hints are given below as to what examiners will consider "good" and "bad" answers.

Good – Brontë compares Heathcliff to *bleak hilly coal country*. This metaphor emphasizes the dark, ugly side of Heathcliff's character.

Bad – Brontë uses many interesting metaphors.

Good – *The larks were silent* at the beginning of Chapter 17 suggests that even the birds are miserable after Catherine's death. Brontë uses pathetic fallacy in this example to convey the sorrow and loneliness felt by Nelly and Edgar.

Bad – Brontë uses many descriptions from nature. These give atmosphere. (This is bad because there isn't an "example" from the story. Even if you can't remember the correct literary term, you will get credit for giving an example to explain what you mean.)

THE EXAM ESSAY

Planning

Writing an excellent essay on a theme from *Wuthering Heights* will challenge your essay writing skills, so it is important to spend some time carefully planning your essay.

1 **Mind Map** your ideas, without worrying about their order yet.
2 **Order** the relevant ideas (the ones that really relate to the question) by numbering them in the order in which you will write the essay.
3 **Gather** your evidence and short quotes.

You could remember this as the **MOG** technique.

Then write the essay, allowing five minutes at the end for checking relevance, and spelling, grammar, and punctuation. **Stick to the question**, and always **back up** your points with evidence in the form of examples and short quotations. Note: You can use "..." for unimportant words missed in a question.

Model answer and essay plan

The next (and final) chapter consists of a model answer to an exam question on *Wuthering Heights*, together with the Mind Map and essay plan used to write it. Don't be disturbed if you think you couldn't write an essay up to this standard yet. This is a top "A"-grade essay, a standard at which to aim. You'll develop your skills if you work at them. Even if you're reading this the night before the exam, you can easily memorize the MOG technique in order to do your personal best.

The model answer and essay plan are good examples for you to follow, but don't try to learn them by heart. It's better to pay close attention to the wording of the question you choose to answer in the exam, and allow Mind Mapping to help you think creatively.

Before reading the answer, you might like to do a plan of your own, then compare it with the example. The numbered points, with comments at the end, show why it's a good answer.

MODEL ANSWER AND ESSAY PLAN

Many authors use the setting of a work of literature to create an appropriate atmosphere and background for the events of the story. This is particularly true of Emily Brontë's novel *Wuthering Heights*.

PLAN

1 Give thesis statement, title, and author of work considered and first impression of the setting
2 Moors
3 Weather and storm
4 The two houses
   a) Wuthering Heights
   b) Thrushcross Grange
5 Conclusion: summing up and referring back to thesis statement

ESSAY

Many great works of literature rely for their power and impact on the vivid depiction of the setting of the story, which can be an integral part of the plot. This is particularly true of Emily Brontë's novel *Wuthering Heights*, which was first published in 1847. Set in northern England in the early years of the nineteenth century, *Wuthering Heights* portrays a world where the bleak landscape and wild weather echo the passionate and tormented lives of the main characters.

Wuthering Heights is both the name of the novel and the house, high on the moors, where much of the drama takes place. In the opening chapter of the book, the reader is introduced to the inhabitants of the house, which is described as being surrounded by "stunted firs" and "gaunt thorns." These

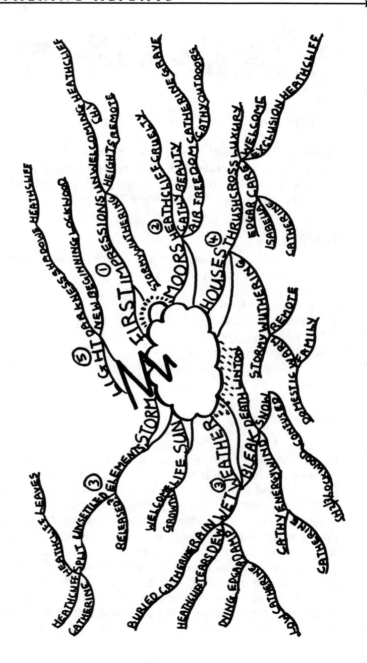

harsh images reflect the miserable people inside the house, who include Hareton, who is stunted because he has never been educated, Catherine, who has lost everything, and Joseph, the servant, who is a miserable and twisted old man. The author mentions the "narrow windows" of the house that make it seem like a fortress to keep the inhabitants locked in and strangers out.

The moors—wild, inhospitable, upland country—which surround the house also reflect the background of what is happening to the characters. The snowstorm in Chapter 3 that traps Lockwood in the Heights demonstrates the changeability and violence of the environment. Two of the main characters, Heathcliff and Catherine, both of whom are wild and passionate, run wild out on the moors to escape the cruelty and neglect of Hindley and Joseph. The moors become linked with the two children, especially Heathcliff, because he is an elemental character, ruled by natural and primitive forces like the moors themselves, which can be full of energy and beauty or wild and cruel. Heathcliff and Catherine love the moors because they are like themselves; Brontë uses the setting of the moors to emphasize their characters and make them vivid to the reader.

Like many authors before and since her time, Brontë makes extensive use of "pathetic fallacy," the idea that the weather echoes the moods and feelings of the characters in the story. An example of this occurs after Catherine's death when, although it is spring, the weather is wet and cold, and "the larks were silent, the young leaves of the early trees 'smitten' and 'blackened'." Brontë describes the day as if it is also in mourning for Catherine. The words "blackened" and "smitten" are dark and depressing, making it seem as if the leaves have also died. Another example is the dramatic storm the night Heathcliff leaves the Heights: "The growling thunder ... the storm came rattling over the Heights in full fury ... there was a violent wind."

The two houses, Wuthering Heights and Thrushcross Grange, are also used by Brontë to echo the atmosphere of the tale. After Hindley has begun to drink and Nelly has left, Wuthering Heights changes from a place that is warm and homelike to being neglected and dirty. Even though there is often trouble and argument at the Heights at the beginning of the story, we still read about warm fires and meals being cooked. Later we hear that the floor is "grey" with dirt, and the pewter dishes have lost their shine. Brontë is suggesting that there is darkness inside her characters, not just in the house. This is emphasized in the description of Heathcliff's bedroom where the curtains and bedding are all torn, and there are dents in the walls, as if he has kicked or punched them. This is a powerful example of the way Heathcliff's violence and destructiveness affects everything around him.

Thrushcross Grange is described as a complete contrast to Wuthering Heights. In Chapter 6, it is "a splendid place carpeted with crimson." Heathcliff finds it beautiful but too "soft," rather like the spoiled young Lintons who live there. It is a world far different from the Heights, far more soothing, luxurious, and protected. Brontë uses this setting to contrast vividly with the Heights.

In the final chapter of the novel, Brontë shows the reader that love and order have won at Wuthering Heights. She creates an atmosphere of peace and harmony by describing "the sweet and warm" spring day and the gardening done by Hareton for Cathy, a symbol of growth and new beginning.

Brontë's superb gift for describing setting and atmosphere to create mood shows the profound effect that depiction of place has on the characters in her novel. Both in her portrayal of place and weather, Brontë has demonstrated the importance of setting in creating an intense and moving novel.

WHAT'S SO GOOD ABOUT IT?

1 The essay opens with a clear thesis statement.
2 Identifies title, author, and setting of the work.
3 Demonstrates how setting affects characters, giving specific examples.
4 Includes brief quotations from the text.
5 Shows how background can be a symbol for an important character.
6 Uses a literary term—pathetic fallacy—to show how the author achieves an effect.
7 Shows a thorough understanding of the text.
8 Uses clear and concise language throughout.
9 Varied and effective use of vocabulary.
10 Obeys the conventions of standard written English.
11 Essay is broken up into clear paragraphs, each dealing with a specific topic.
12 Comes to a neat and logical conclusion echoing the main theme of the essay.

GLOSSARY OF LITERARY TERMS

accent a combination of how people pronounce words (for example, Joseph's *frough morn tuh neeght*), which Emily Brontë suggests by spelling, and their intonation (ups and downs in the pitch of their voices).

alliteration repetition of a sound at the beginning of words; for example, ladies' lips.

context the social and historical influences on the author.

dialect local words used in speech (for example, Joseph's *hearken* for "hear").

foreshadowing an indirect warning of things to come, often through **imagery**.

image a word picture used to make an idea come alive; a **metaphor**, **simile**, or **personification** (see separate entries).

imagery the kind of word picture used to make an idea come alive.

irony (1) where the author or characters say the opposite of what they really think, or pretend ignorance of the true facts, usually for the sake of humor or ridicule; (2) where events turn out in what seems a particularly inappropriate way, as if mocking human effort.

metaphor a description of a thing as if it were something essentially different but also in some way similar; for example, *her eyes radiant with cloudless pleasure* (Chapter 21).

pathetic fallacy similar to **personification**, it gives human feelings and emotions to nature; for example, the *growling thunder* in Chapter 9 makes the storm seem angry about Heathcliff's departure from Wuthering Heights.

personification a description of something (such as fate) as if it were a person.

prose language in which, unlike verse, there is no set number of syllables in a line, and no rhyming.

rhetorical question one asked for effect or as a figure of speech, expecting no answer; for example, Heathcliff, *How the devil is he so like?* Chapter 31).

setting the place in which the action occurs, usually affecting the atmosphere; for example, the moor.

simile a comparison of two things that are different in most ways but similar in one important way; for example, Heathcliff speaking of Linton: *I'll crush his ribs in like a rotten hazelnut* (Chapter 11).

structure how the plot is organized.

theme an idea explored by an author; for example, death.

viewpoint how the story is told; for example, through action, or in discussion between minor characters.

NDEX

books 21, 34, 43, 51, 60, 66, 67, 68, 73
Catherine
    character 12, 28, 31, 33, 34, 36–7, 38, 40
    and Edgar 34, 37, 42, 43, 47
    and Edgar/Heathcliff conflict 36, 37, 38, 39, 40–1, 42, 48
    and Heathcliff 28, 30, 32, 33, 34, 36, 37, 38, 39, 40, 48
    and illness/death 38, 42, 43, 45, 48, 49
    and Isabella 40
    power after death 28, 48, 65, 70
Cathy
    character 16, 49, 51, 52, 55, 57, 58–9, 60, 66, 67, 68
    and Hareton 56, 60, 67, 68, 69
    and Heathcliff 62, 65, 69
    and Linton 53, 55, 58, 59
Catherine and Cathy, comparison 47, 52, 53, 58, 66
childhood 19, 30, 51
circularity (cycle) *see* repetition
currant bushes 69

death and sleep 19–20, 28, 31, 32, 35, 37, 38, 43, 48, 49, 53, 56, 61, 65, 66, 70–1

Edgar 12–13, 32, 36–7, 39, 42, 43, 47, 60
education 32, 34, 41
eyes 40, 42, 47

Hareton 16, 35, 41, 50, 51, 52, 56, 57, 60, 66, 67, 68
Heathcliff
    character 10–12, 26, 30, 34, 36, 40, 41, 45, 46, 47, 49, 50, 51, 56, 65, 70
    and Catherine 28, 30, 32, 33, 36, 38, 47, 48, 65, 70
    and Cathy 27, 56, 62, 69
    and Edgar 39, 49, 45, 63
    and Hareton 51, 55-6, 57, 67, 69, 70
    and Hindley 30, 32, 34, 38, 40, 50
    and Isabella 40, 41, 46
    and Linton 50, 54, 55, 56, 57, 61
Hindley 12, 30, 32, 33, 35, 37, 40

imagery 41
imprisonment and freedom 18, 42, 43, 45, 47, 49, 52, 58, 62, 63, 68
inheritance 49, 50, 54, 55, 65
irony 54, 56, 61, 81
Isabella 14, 32, 41, 46, 48, 50, 53

jealousy 40
Joseph 10, 27, 31, 45, 52, 53, 58, 60, 68, 69

Linton 53, 55–6, 57, 58, 59, 60, 62, 63, 66
Lockwood 26, 27, 28, 29, 34, 67, 71
love 17–18, 37, 39, 41, 59

marriage 54, 62, 63
metaphors 45, 47, 51, 52, 57, 81
Mind Mapping vii–viii
MOG technique 73

nature 18, 28, 39, 45, 49, 62
Nelly 14, 34, 48–9, 57, 58, 62, 68, 71

outsiders 19, 26, 30, 34

pathetic fallacy 74, 75
plot
    outline 4–6
    revision 7–8
portrait 63

religion 21, 28, 31
repetition 41, 49, 52, 54, 61, 63, 66
rhetorical questions 45, 82

simile 36, 82
social class 20, 27, 32, 41, 42, 52, 56, 33
starvation 43
storms 31, 39
style and language 22, 26, 27, 40, 45, 47, 49, 51, 52, 54, 56–7, 58, 60, 61, 62, 66
supernatural 21, 42, 70–1
symbolism 22, 63, 69

theme
    definition 12
themes 17–21
Thrushcross Grange 32

violence 36, 37, 39, 43, 45, 48, 50

weather 27, 31, 58, 62
windows and doors 56, 62, 68
Wuthering Heights 26, 68, 69